ENERGY

WORK

Also by Robert Bruce

Astral Dynamics

Practical Psychic Self-Defense

Master Astral Projection (Llewellyn Worldwide, MN, coauthored with Brian Mercer)

Mastering Astral Projection CD Companion (Llewellyn Worldwide, MN, coauthored with Brian Mercer)

ENERGY
WORK

The Secret of Healing and Spiritual Development

ROBERT BRUCE

HAMPTON ROADS
PUBLISHING COMPANY, INC.

Cover design by Frame25 Productions
Cover art by Phil Kestell, c/o Shutterstock

Hampton Roads Publishing Company, Inc.
1125 Stoney Ridge Road
Charlottesville, VA 22902

434-296-2772
fax: 434-296-5096
e-mail: hrpc@hrpub.com
www.hrpub.com

If you are unable to order this book from your local
bookseller, you may order directly from the publisher.
Call 1-800-766-8009, toll-free.

Library of Congress Cataloging-in-Publication Data

Bruce, Robert, 1955-
Energy work : the secret of healing and spiritual development / Robert Bruce.
p. cm.
Summary: "Energy Work incorporates thought-form imaging, intention, elemental properties, self-healing practices, and essential grounding exercises to put
readers in touch with their energy bodies. Presented in non-esoteric language and
embellished with easy-to-follow illustrations, this is an invaluable guide for anyone seeking to take charge of their energy body, transcend spiritual plateaus, and
escalate their evolution as a spiritual being"--Provided by publisher.
Includes bibliographical references.
ISBN 978-1-57174-540-8 (5.5 x 8.5 tp : alk. paper)
1. Astral body. 2. Spiritual healing. 3. Spiritual life. I. Title.
BF1389.A7B79 2007
133.9'5--dc22
2007007367
ISBN 978-1-57174-540-8
10 9 8 7 6 5 4 3
Printed on acid-free paper in the United States

To Patricia, my sensitive, energy-wise friend, whose loving encouragement and healing counsel were indispensable ingredients for the creation of this book.

And in loving memory of Taryn . . . rest easy little princess.

Contents

NEW History

How did this system of energy work originate, and how was it developed?

In 1994, I discovered the Internet and began helping many people around the world with astral projection and energy work issues. Among these people were two young men who had been blind since birth. They did not know sight and, therefore, could not visualize at all. As all astral projection and energy work techniques rely on visualization, they were stumped. Focusing on what I had to work with, I came up with the idea of using the sense of touch for an astral projection technique. I called the underlying method body awareness tactile imaging. The idea was, if they used body awareness to *feel* themselves climbing hand over hand up a rope, this would help trigger an astral projection exit. I road tested this and found it very effective. I called this "the rope" projection technique.

A few months later I was relaxing by my fire in the evening when an idea surfaced that had been brewing for weeks: As body awareness tactile imaging was so effective as a projection technique, it might also stimulate the energy body in other ways. I reached down with my body awareness hands and focused on my feet. I reasoned that as there are primary energy centers (major Chakras), there must also be smaller energy centers. The feet seemed a good place to start. I moved my point of body awareness to focus on various parts of my body. This caused some mild energy sensations, but nothing major happened. Then I focused on my right big toe and moved my point of body awareness back and forth through it. Within seconds this caused strong buzzing and throbbing sensations. I increased my attention and the sensations grew even stronger. Excited, I tried this on other parts of my feet and other areas of my body. The energy sensations this produced were mind-blowing. I sat there flabbergasted, realizing that I had discovered a major secret of energy work.

I continued working like this for months, several hours a day, feeling my way through my energy body a fraction of an inch at a time. I kept extensive notes and sketches and before long a rudimentary model of the human energy body emerged, along with an improved understanding of how it all worked. I then wrote an energy work tutorial called "NEW Energy Ways" (NEW for short) and released it on the Internet. This sparked a flood of feedback from energy workers and astral projectors all over the world. My continued personal exploration, plus helping others with energy-related problems and issues, progressively enhanced my understanding of the human energy body and how it works.

Body Awareness Tactile Imaging energy work became the foundation of all my work. I realized the importance of the energy body and how it is fundamentally related to all spiritual abilities and phenomena. Stimulating and developing the energy body is key to everything metaphysical. All my books, starting with the publication of *Astral Dynamics* by Hampton Roads Publishing Company in 1999, reflected this by presenting energy work tutorials.

I began presenting workshops and seminars in 2003. The instant feedback gained from personally working with groups of people was invaluable. This greatly improved my understanding of the energy body and stimulation and development practices. I learned something new from every group I taught, and this continues today. Body awareness tactile imaging energy work has come a long way since 1994. It has steadily grown into the book you are now holding. However, I will always consider this system to be *a work in progress*. As my explorations continue, I am always discovering new and exciting ways to use energy.

Acknowledgments

My gratitude to Caroline Needham, for her fantastic illustrations; to Jesse Bruce, for his illustrative contributions; to Benjamin Bruce, for his loving support and psychological advice; to James and Kathlene and Teresa and Ginny, for being there.

My appreciation to: Donni Hakanson, Kim Fitzpatrick-Bruce, Gerik Cionsky, Jeff Valair, Patty Mowery, Brian Mercer, Bob Felix and Marina Mattocks, Donald McGlinn, Peter Eardley, Joseph Woods, Kurt Allen, Marcia Hugall, Catherine Curran, Dan Fritz, India Supera, Richard and Michelle Kaplowitz, Maureen Caudill, David Elam, Jordan Eldridge, Penny and Ullani, Mitch Kibblewhite, Errol Drane, May, Beth, Alison, and Suzy.

My gratitude to Frank DeMarco, Tania Seymour, Bob Friedman, and all the wonderful staff at Hampton Roads Publishing Co., for their encouragement, patience, and professional advice during the production of this book.

I also acknowledge the many persons I have discussed energy work with over the years that, without knowing, helped to evolve my energetic methods to their current standards; and the sea of smiling faces of my many students, who by allowing me to teach and experiment gave me wonderful ideas. In particular, a big group hug goes to my 2006 Montana Feathered Pipe Ranch workshop students!

Special thanks to my adventurous friend, Keith Alderslade, for his reasonably sane counsel on matters having little to do with this book but that helped all the same.

Introduction

Welcome to my world of energy work! I wish I had held this book in my hand 30 years ago, as my life would have been so much easier. The good news is that you are now holding this book. May your life benefit greatly from the ideas it offers.

Pure consciousness is energy, and energy knows no boundaries. Imagination, emotion, intention, and energetic actions are all expressions of consciousness and energy. "Where your attention goes your energy flows" is a fundamental principle of energy work. And your energetic actions will always be shaped by your thoughts, with exactly the properties you imagine and intend them to contain.

The energy work system presented here is easy to do and extremely effective. Anyone can do this. There are no age or health limitations, and no previous experience or skill is needed. Most people will experience noticeable energy movement sensations during early exercises. These are physical sensations, not just imaginary feelings. Progress is rapid once the basic principles and methods are grasped.

Energy work has many practical uses. It improves physical health and self-healing and accelerates all aspects of spiritual and psychic development. Running energy through your energy body stimulates your physical body's own powerful self-healing mechanisms and connects you with your higher self. "Where your attention goes your energy flows" applies to how pain works. Pain draws attention to an injury and focuses your body's self-repair energies. The energy work system presented here allows you to activate this same self-healing mechanism without having to experience pain, and to focus your energies in areas you want to stimulate and develop spiritually.

Energy Work is a collection of simple practices based on focused body awareness actions. Starting with a set of exercises that will have you feeling energy quickly, it builds step-by-step into a complete system for stimulating and developing your energy body.

The system presented here was developed from scratch. This began with an accidental discovery, followed by years of experimentation (see the preface for more details). Learning this system will put you in touch with your energy body and greatly expand your spiritual horizons. This provides a wonderful on-ramp with which to approach the greater spiritual reality and to evolve as a spiritual being.

My previous books contain elements of this energy work system, previously called *NEW Energy Ways*, as this is the cornerstone of my work. Since all spiritual techniques and practices involve the energy body in one way or another, it should be obvious that any spiritual practice can be enhanced by more effective techniques. But more effective does not mean more difficult; just the opposite. My way of teaching is to first impart a simple understanding of the energy, and then to expand on this one step at a time. Spiritual complexities can be explored later.

The descriptions of the energy body, meridian energy lines, and energetic structures given throughout this book are based largely upon my own observations gained through the practice of energy work. This book focuses on *doing* energy work rather than on *discussing* its technical and esoteric complexities. With this in mind, complex theory and explanations are kept to a minimum. And with that said, it is time to begin an amazing journey, a journey of learning by doing, which is surely the only way to truly *know* anything.

ONE

Your Energy Body

Your energy body is the underlying subtle energy template of your physical body. There are various traditional and contemporary approaches to energy work, but all aspire to the same end: to stimulate and develop the human energy body. The goal is to evolve spiritually, and in so doing, to become a healthier and a more dynamic human being. This book introduces a powerful new energy work system that is both simple and effective.

The importance of the human energy body to health and vitality has been known for thousands of years. Life energy has been given many labels, including Chi, Prana, Huna, Odic Force, Orgone, et cetera. It has been utilized by many practices including Chi Kung, Tai Chi, Yoga, Kung Fu, Acupuncture, Reiki, Reflexology, Pranic Healing, Quantum Touch, et cetera. Any system that involves subtle energy use, energy manipulation, or healing can be enhanced by incorporating the body awareness–based energy movement principles that are the foundation of this book.

The more vital energy you have, the more alive you become on every level: physical, mental, emotional, creative, and spiritual. Whether you seek to improve your traditional practices, to improve your health, or develop spiritual and psychic abilities, effective energy work is the key to success.

Human activity involves energy in every molecule, bone, muscle, and organ—even while just thinking or sleeping. Every thought, organ function, and physical movement involves masses of bioelectrical and biochemical signals coursing throughout your body. All electrical activity generates electromagnetic fields. A biomagnetic field is an electromagnetic field that is produced by a living being. Some of these fields are subtle and difficult to detect, but this does not mean they are unimportant. The strongest human biomagnetic field is produced by the heart, which can be detected at a distance of more than 15 feet (five meters). The energy produced by healers and energy workers has also been measured by similar equipment and shown to be a significant force (Oschman and Pert 2000).

Subtle energy flows through the human energy body in many ways. Besides from physical sources like food and drink, two primary sources are the energy generated by our planet and the air we breathe. Subtle life energy comes from the atmosphere, solar energy, and the cosmic energies of the universe. Energies are also exchanged between people and all living things. On the subatomic level, all matter is energy. The entire universe is, in fact, an infinite expression of energy and consciousness. And on the energy level, all living and nonliving things are intimately connected.

What Is the Energy Body?

Every cell of your body is alive with bioelectrical activity that produces biomagnetic fields. Beneath this activity exist the layers of subtle and spiritual energy fields that comprise the human energy body. This subtle body is every bit as complex as its physical counterpart, even though its subtle and spiritual structures are difficult to detect.

To date, the only tool sensitive enough to perceive the more subtle human energies is a sensitive human being. To truly grasp this, you must learn how to feel energy for yourself by feeling and moving your own energy. A major goal of this book is to demonstrate this to you. Only when you feel your own energy will you truly know that you have an energy body. And only then will you be able to truly work with energy. This is not difficult, as I will soon show.

The human energy body overlays the physical body like a template, but parts of it also exist independently. In the case of limb amputations, the underlying energy body parts continue to function. Occasionally, a Kirlian photograph (a high voltage coronal discharge photograph) will show parts of subjects on film that have been lost or removed previously (e.g., amputated fingers or plant parts).

The human energy body has multiple layers and energy centers. Energy centers (also called Chakras) are like the vital organs of the energy body. This includes the seven primary energy centers (major Chakras), hundreds of secondary energy centers, three energy storage centers, and dense areas of tertiary centers (tiny energy exchange pores). There is also a central channel (Sushumna) running up the center of the body, with two major energy conduits (called Ida and Pingala) winding up either side. This structure is traditionally represented by the caduceus symbol (staff of Hermes).

The human energy body is a complex, multilayered structure. When one first approaches energy work, a simple approach is best. The following illustration shows the basic structures of the human energy body, including primary centers, storage centers, and energy exchange areas. We will discuss this further as we progress.

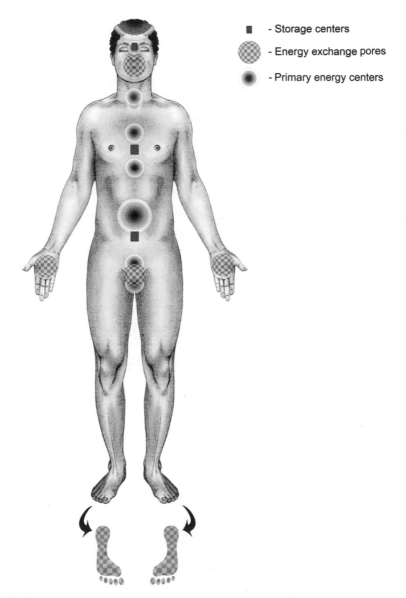

■ - Storage centers

▨ - Energy exchange pores

● - Primary energy centers

It is unnecessary to memorize a host of exotic Eastern terms and concepts to actually work with the energy body. I use Western descriptive terms wherever possible. This makes discussing and working with the energy body easier. Every part of the physical body is also part of the energy body. This will become clear as you work through the exercises.

What Is Energy Work?

How you think and feel profoundly effects your energy body. If you feel happy, your energy body expands and empowers you. But if you are sad, your energy body shrinks and drains your vitality and enthusiasm for life. Energy work improves and balances health and vitality on all levels. An amplified sense of body awareness and increased energy flow also encourage your higher spiritual aspects to become more actively engaged in your life.

There are many ways this can be achieved. "All roads lead to Rome," but some roads are shorter than others. Traditional approaches involve various combinations of visualization, physical movement and stretching, posturing and breathing, and/or chanting or toning, all of which stimulate subtle energy flow in different ways. The typical New Age approach involves mainly visualization and relaxation exercises. Visualization is, however, difficult for many people because it is generally misunderstood. I teach the secrets of effective visualization in the next chapter. Everyone can visualize perfectly once they learn how.

The energy work taught in this book is a *tactile* imaging system that does not require visualization. Tactile imaging involves focusing the awareness of your physical body—your body awareness—on a specific point in your body, and then moving that focal point. This stimulates the energy body very effectively. This is simple to learn and anyone can do it. This is not only simpler than any other system, but it is significantly more effective.

The underlying principles of body awareness energy movement and tactile imaging can be found in all Eastern energy-based systems. At a glance this is not obvious, perhaps because of the difficulties involved in translating Eastern esoteric concepts. I think that the use of body awareness actions to stimulate the energy body is a given in the Eastern traditions that just does not translate well. I have spoken to many teachers of traditional practices on this matter. All have seen my point and have adjusted their teachings accordingly, simply by clarifying the importance of body awareness actions. Students then progress much faster than they would have otherwise. This is because once a student learns how to feel and move subtle energy, the traditional system they are learning becomes more accessible and doable as everything clicks neatly into place.

My eldest son, Benjamin, is a psychologist. He has practiced tactile imaging energy work for several years, besides studying various systems such as Zen, Tao, Yoga, et cetera. A few years back, he signed up for a course on Iron Shirt Chi Kung. He was told that most students would start feeling significant levels of energy movement if they practiced every day for a year. But during the first day of instruction, Benjamin was feeling major energy movement. (His instructors could not understand such rapid progress, and they were not open to Benjamin's explanation.) I have heard many similar reports over the years.

Why Do Energy Work?

Normally, many of the structures within the human energy body are virtually dormant. They function at a level sufficient for normal physical existence, but on a very low level in a spiritual sense. These structures and energy centers can awaken accidentally, often causing spontaneous psychic experiences, or they can be brought out of dormancy by spiritual practices and energy work.

The benefits of energy work come on every level. It encourages the physical body to function better, to maintain and repair itself more efficiently, and to resist disease. The ability to work directly with your energy body allows you to stimulate your body's own self-healing mechanisms in specific ways to target injured or diseased areas.

Vital energies flow through every part of your body. This is every bit as important to life as blood. Just as your physical body will adapt and change in response to lifestyle, exercise, and diet, so will your energy body—for better or worse. When you do energy work, your energy body will be excited into higher levels of activity. And just like working out regularly in a gym improves your physical body, this progressively improves the fitness and functionality of your energy body.

Psychic and spiritual development are heavily dependent upon energy body activity. Everyone has dormant or partial psychic abilities and everyone has great spiritual potential, but very few people get to realize these things in any significant way. Body awareness based–energy work methods allow for the specific targeting of energy conduits and primary energy centers. By exercising these, they can be activated, developed, and evolved. This translates into actual spiritual development and evolution.

The human energy body contains seven primary energy centers (also called Chakras or psychic centers), hundreds of secondary energy centers, three storage centers (also called Tan Tians), and thousands of tertiary centers (energy exchange pores). All of these centers—primary, secondary, and tertiary—are interconnected through myriad subtle energy pathways. Central to the energy body is a tubelike channel structure. The human energy body is every bit as complex as the inner workings of the human physical body and its nervous system, with which it is intimately related.

Note: My intention here is to impart a workable rule of thumb understanding of the energy body. Descriptions are based largely upon my own observations. Western descriptive terms are used wherever possible. I am not attempting to agree or disagree with any particular tradition or school of thought.

Vital energy is produced in the physical body through the digestion of food and drink. *Subtle energies* are also taken in through the hands and feet, breathing, and environmental and social interactions with the world around us. Subtle energies enter the body and circulate through networks of subtle energy pathways and energy centers. Energy centers absorb and transform the qualities of subtle energies that are available to or passing through them. They can be likened to subtle transformers, changing the quality and

7

frequency of subtle energies to suit a variety of needs on all levels of existence.

Primary Energy Centers

Your emotions are the most noticeable link with primary energy

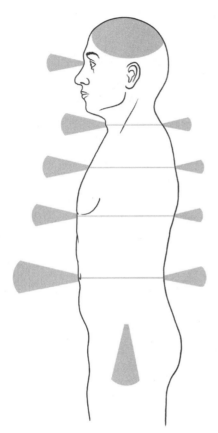

center activity. Uplifting music can cause tingling energy surges to rise through your back. Sadness can cause great heaviness. A sudden shock can cause your throat to dry out instantly. Fear and excitement can cause goose bumps or make your hair stand up. Intense fear can cause your bowels to loosen and your legs to go weak. Mental pressure can cause tension headaches. A broken heart can cause depression and a physical ache in your heart. Falling in love can cause the sensation of butterflies in your stomach. There are as many sensations relating to primary center activity as there are emotions and emotionally charged situations.

The seven primary energy centers are as follows: the base center, navel center, solar plexus center, heart center, throat center, brow center, and crown center. These are the major subtle organs of the energy body. They are involved with every aspect of human existence. They are always active on some level. These centers are responsible for all emotional, psychic, and spiritual senses. Primary energy centers will be dealt with in more detail later in this book.

Secondary Energy Centers

Secondary energy centers are similar to primary energy centers, but they are much smaller and have simpler functions. These vary in size and are placed throughout the flesh and bone of the whole physical body. These energy centers and their meridian connections are well documented in traditional Chinese acupuncture systems.

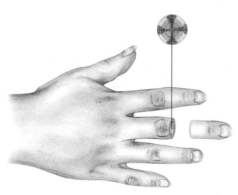

This diagram represents a typical skeletal-type secondary energy center in a finger joint. These types of energy centers have four poles each and a central connecting core. Each pole is a small vortexlike energy structure that flowers on the surface of the skin and directly above the joint. These poles are connected to larger internal conduits, which run through the core and marrow of all bones. When energy flows strongly through core channels, it can overstimulate physical nerves and cause tingling, surging sensations deep in the bone marrow. These sensations are particularly noticeable in the arms and legs. Skeletal-type secondary centers exist in every joint of the human body, small and large.

Many important secondary centers exist throughout the body, in flesh and organs and ganglia, all joined together by subtle energy connec-

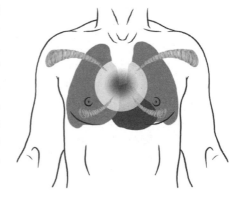

tions. A good example of this is found around the heart center structure. The diagram below shows robust energy conduits connecting through the arms and shoulders and into the lungs. (The entire heart center structure and its connections are vastly more complex than is shown here.)

The upper conduits connect the heart center with the arms. The lower conduits connect with the lungs. These conduits are paired, feeding from the back as well as from the front. People who are body awareness sensitive will be able to feel these structures when they are active. The heart center also has branches connecting to other areas (e.g., to the throat).

Tertiary Energy Exchange Pores

Energy exchange pores are tiny energy centers with simple functions, like the millions of sweat pores that cover the surface of the skin. The main function of these tiny energy centers is to exchange subtle energy with other people and with the environment. The surface of the skin is covered with these, but they are highly concentrated in several areas: the soles of the feet, the palms of the hands, the nose and nasal passages, the eyes and ears, the lungs, the mouth, the lips, the tongue, and the genitals. Energy exchange pores are very sensitive and have the ability to tune into and sense subtle energy fields. The hands in particular can be used as fine sensory organs to feel energy fields.

Energy Storage Centers

The human energy body has three major energy storage centers, where different qualities of energies are accumulated. These are different from the primary energy centers that share the same general areas, although these are, of course, all energetically connected. The storage centers are shown here.

The Sub-Navel Center: This sits midway between the belly button and the pubic line, two inches inside the average body. Its function is to store raw physical vitality. When stimulated, this center produces a fluttering, bubbling energy movement sensation often an inch or two to the side of the central point or pubic line. This is not to be confused with gas movement in the intestines.

The Sub-Heart Center: This sits in the middle of the chest between the nipples, two inches inside the average body. Its function is to store raw emotional energy.

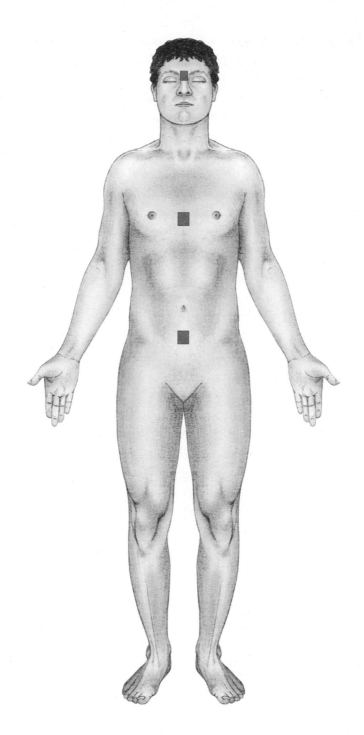

The Sub-Brow Center: This sits between the eyebrows in the center of the brow, just inside the skull. Its function is to store raw mental/psychic energy.

I have greatly simplified the description of the nature of energy storage centers to make them more understandable. Of the three energy storage centers, the most important to fill is the Sub-Navel storage center. When this is full, it can be said to overflow naturally conditioned energy into the Sub-Heart, and then into the Sub-Brow.

Group experiments have taught me that excessively filling the two higher storage centers in the heart and brow is unwise. This can disrupt the energy body and cause predictable problems, including emotional, mental, and psychic instability. There are no safe shortcuts here.

The Central Channel

The central channel (called Sushumna, an Eastern term) flows vertically through the middle of the body, from the base center (centered in the perineum) to the middle of the crown center (middle top of head). An energy field can be felt extending and mushrooming from the central channel above the head, varying from a few inches to a couple of feet above. Two major energy conduits weave through the central channel, called Ida on the left side and Pingala on the right side, to use the Eastern terms. The roots of these rise up through the legs and into the base center structure. These conduits then weave up the central channel, crossing through each primary energy center as they rise. They pass through the mouth cavity at the back of the mouth, each side near the second rear molars.

The spine and spinal cord are intimately related to the central channel, but the physical area occupied by the central channel is central not to the spine, but to the torso and head. The central channel feels to be about four inches in diameter for the average person, narrowing slightly as it passes through the neck. The outer part of this structure feels *magnetic*. This rotates clockwise and then counterclockwise. I have observed rotational changes happening at various

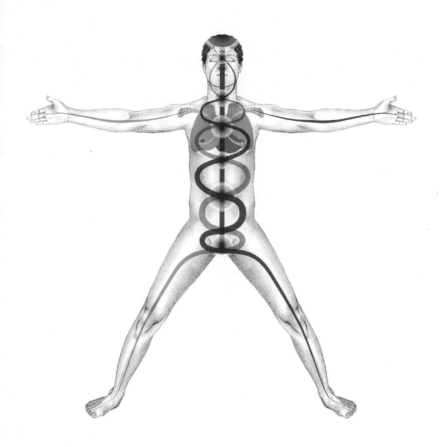

intervals—10 to 60 minutes or more. The timing and duration of the rotational phase varies from person to person and in response to changes in consciousness and physical activity.

The central channel rotation is not consistent. It will naturally rotate longer in one direction and shorter in the other. This rotation can be perceived with body awareness perceptions by sensitive people. This change in rotation appears related to the natural flow of energy up through the legs, with legs alternating in dominance. Energy flows up through one leg at a time. When the dominance of leg energy flow changes, there is a short period of turbulence in the central channel as it stops and reverses direction. If you are tuned into and sensing the central channel during a changeover, some moments of dizziness may be felt during this event; otherwise it generally happens unnoticed.

The inner parts of the central channel feel *electric* to body aware-ness senses. The coiling and uncoiling of myriad delicate energy threads can be sensed inside the central channel as it turns. There is also a subtle energy pulse moving through the central channel.

The first step in becoming aware of the central channel is to become aware of the sensations it causes inside you. Once these are perceived, awareness of this structure will grow. These sensations are felt as a kind of mild, churning vertigo inside the stomach and chest. This can be like the sinking feelings you get in your stomach when an elevator starts moving or when you miss a step. There are correspon-ding sensations in the head, arms, and legs that relate to the flow of energy through the central channel.

Central channel–related sensations respond to physical move-ments and postures, and to thoughts and breathing. Some thoughts will cause these sensations to flare, and some will cause them to diminish. Body awareness actions, like the central channel bounce, will tend to clear this structure of energy blockages and make it more sensitive and noticeable.

The Aura Field

Activity within the human energy body generates a strong but subtle energy field that extends some distance from the surface of the physical body. This distance varies depending on energy body health, development, and activity. Imagine an egg shape enclosing the phys-ical body about one yard (one meter) thick and you have the idea. (The illustration is not to scale.)

Each primary energy center projects colored energy into the aura field. The base center is red, the navel is orange, the solar plexus is yellow, the heart is green, the throat is blue, the brow is indigo to pur-ple, and the crown is violet. This often creates a bandlike appearance in the human aura if viewed clairvoyantly. For average persons, these colors usually blend and create a general hue, which changes depend-ing on their emotions and the activity of individual primary centers. The human aura can be perceived, but it is not composed of any type or frequency of light. It is a complex and subtle energy field projected from the front and rear of a person. The human aura can be perceived in two basic ways: with aura sight and with clairvoyant sight.

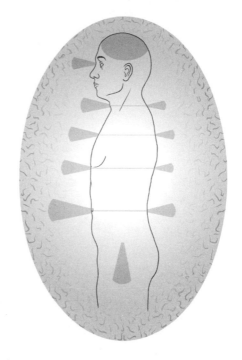

Aura sight is achieved by the eyes and the brow center working together. The eyes and the brow center are both connected to the sight center of the brain. The eyes help the brow center focus on and perceive the aura. Aura colors are seen super-imposed over normal vision. Aura sight involves observing a subject with peripheral vision, by gazing slightly to the side of a subject and unfocusing the eyes. This gaze must be held, as the aura will disappear if it is focused upon directly. Clairvoyance is a significantly higher level of visual psychic ability, and this involves direct perception by the brow center. With visual clairvoyance, the eyes can be open or shut.

The basic colors of the human aura are fairly consistent when viewed with aura sight from any angle. However, to view the deeper structures of the energy body requires clairvoyance. These structures are most visible when a subject is observed from directly in front. They are less clear when viewed from the rear, and difficult to see at all when viewed from the side.

TWO

Visualization and Breath Work

This chapter shows how you can visualize perfectly, right now. Your sense of touch and awareness of your own body, your sense of body awareness, are essential for effective energy work. This chapter introduces the principles of body awareness energy work and explains how tactile imaging dynamically stimulates the energy body.

Visualization and Imagination

The techniques in this book do not involve *visualization*. Instead, they rely on a nonvisual system called tactile imaging. This is easy to learn and to use, and far more effective than visualization-based methods. All energy work and spiritual development practices rely largely on visualization, so difficulties in this area create serious problems.

Most people have problems visualizing, and many believe they cannot visualize at all. But visualization is a natural ability that everyone can do perfectly immediately. Visualization is *not* a visual skill. You do not have to see anything visual in your mind when you visualize. If you do see something, it is a mind's eye vision (clairvoyance) or an awake, lucid dream-type experience.

Visualization is pure imagination, pure fantasy. Every child can do this perfectly. A visualization exercise or led meditation is exactly the same as any other fantasy, where memory is used to build a fictional scenario in the mind's eye. It may be full of sights, sounds, smells, tastes, textures, and feelings, but nothing is actually *seen* visually.

Memory plays an important part in imagination and visualization. Have you ever replayed past actions in your mind, in your mind's eye, to help you find a lost item? Replaying or re-creating events—whether real or fictitious—involves the constructive use of imagination. This is perfect visualization, and everyone has the natural ability to do this perfectly—right now!

The very word *visual*-ization is a big part of the problem, especially when used to describe inner practices like meditation and energy work. This problem is increased by the visual terms commonly used to describe nonvisual experiences, which includes all nonvisual psychic perceptions. This is compounded by people who psychically perceive things (not actually seeing anything visually) habitually using visual terms like "I saw," "I see," and "I am seeing." This is often misleading to students. More accurate terms like "I sense," "I feel," and "I perceive" are less confusing.

There is a hidden ego component in the above problem. In our competitive society, it sounds far more convincing if psychic perceptions are stated as being visual experiences. It can be related to how eyewitness testimonies are taken as evidence superior to gut instincts and feelings. "I sensed this" or "I perceived this" doesn't sound as convincing as "I saw this!" I cannot see the popular use of these terms changing, but clearer explanations and instructions can help overcome the problems they cause for students.

The visualization problem is worsened in any group where the teacher and a few students happen to be naturally clairvoyant.

Clairvoyants do see what they visualize in a visual mind's eye way. They often do not realize that this does not apply to the vast majority of people, and so students get the impression that visual visualization ability is the norm. This can lead to students believing that they are deficient in this area. This misunderstanding totally stunts student development. Many students in this situation will pretend that they can see what they are told to visualize, lest the rest of the class think they are deficient. This whole problem can be overcome by giving more accurate explanations.

Some people will actually see things *visually* in their mind's eyes during visualization exercises. This often happens when deep physical/mental relaxation is involved. This can produce the mind awake/body asleep state (also called the trance state). This can activate visual clairvoyant abilities. The dream mind can also become active and produce visual mind's eye imagery. But teachers and students should never assume that mind's eye visual ability is the norm for all of their students.

Body Awareness and Tactile Imaging

The key to effective energy work is developing tactile awareness of your physical body. This stimulates the flow of vital energy and encourages spiritual development. Many traditional systems utilize this principle. Zen practices, for example, stress developing an acute awareness of one's physical body and how it interacts with the physical world in every possible way. Walking meditation is a good example, where one learns how to walk consciously and be aware of every shift of gravity, muscle movement, and tactile contact. This includes wearing thin-soled, moccasin-type shoes to heighten tactile contact with the ground.

Your natural center of awareness rests in your eyes, as sight is the strongest sense if you are sighted. This is the window through which you observe the physical world. But your center of conscious awareness is not restricted to your eyes. Your mind does not reside inside your head, but includes your entire physical body. The eyes are just the habitual focus of consciousness.

Your conscious attention, focused on a specific part of your body, energetically stimulates that part. When you move this focal point of body awareness through your body, you also stimulate the underlying energy body structures of that area. Body awareness movement causes direct energy body stimulation. This is tactile imaging. In a similar way, energy can be moved throughout your body, and specific parts and energy centers can thus be targeted and stimulated.

Tactile imaging is the underlying principle of all energy work and development systems, although it is never explained this way. Grasping this is key to success or failure with any energy work system. A major goal of this book is to make the principles of energy work understandable and accessible.

How Tactile Imaging Affects the Physical and Energy Bodies

The focus of body awareness attention in any part of the physical body—say in the hand—causes the nerves in that hand to charge up and prepare for physical movement. If movement does not occur—if the focal point of body awareness continually shifts as tactile imaging actions are performed—these nerves discharge. So, when body awareness is brushed back and forth through the hand, the nerves there are continually charging and discharging. This increases bioelectrical activity and causes some unusual physical sensations.

The bioelectrical activity caused by tactile imaging actions in the physical body causes a corresponding biomagnetic disturbance in the substance of the energy body. This is like a subtle energy ripple wave effect. The intensity and motion of this subtle energy wave varies according to the location and intensity of the tactile imaging action being performed. Some areas of the energy body, such as the hands and feet, are more sensitive than others. This relates partly to the density of nerves in the physical body and partly to subtle energy body structures sharing the same space.

Tactile imaging actions can be performed on the surface of the physical body, deep inside the physical body, or even outside the physical body. They can also be extended further out to affect the energy bodies of other persons.

Tactile imaging causes some unusual physical sensations. While the type and intensity vary from person to person, the most common include feelings of tightness, heaviness, fuzziness, thickness, tingling, buzzing, fluttering, fizzing, mild cramping, and warm or cool sensations. Again, these sensations are caused by increased energy movement stimulating nerves in the physical body.

Strong energy movement-related physical sensations are common for beginners, especially during the first few weeks of energy work. These sensations will always abate with practice, as the energy body and the nerves of the physical body adapt to higher levels of energy movement and bioelectrical activity.

Little or no sensation during early energy work can indicate three things: a healthy or already well-developed energy body, or a sluggish energy body with energy blockages, or ineffective tactile imaging actions. Out of the thousands of people I have taught this energy work to, I have come across only a very small group of people who felt no sensations. However, in all cases where people persevere with energy work, the energy body eventually responds and produces normal energy movement sensations.

Practice

The following simple exercises show how to focus body awareness in different parts of your body. This is essential body awareness training for tactile imaging.

To prepare yourself, sit in a chair with your shoes off and do not cross your legs. Eliminate distractions like music, tight clothing, et cetera. Close your eyes, take a few deep breaths to settle yourself, and begin. Lightly rub or scratch the specified areas of your body as necessary. Use a pen or ruler for this if you cannot reach. This helps target specific areas so that body awareness can be focused more accurately. The scratching and rubbing method of targeting is discontinued later.

Key Point: When you focus on any area of your body, it helps if you imagine that you are trying to feel slight changes in air temperature and air movement there.

Rub or lightly scratch your left kneecap, causing a mild tingling to help target this with your body awareness. Feel for this tingling area with your body awareness, with your sense of touch and feel. Feel for more of your knee and become more aware of it as a joint. Feel around it, on the sides and back, and then move your point of body awareness around it several times, as if bandaging your knee. Your center of body awareness is now focused entirely in your left knee.

Shift your point of body awareness slowly down your left leg to your big toe. Scratch or wiggle the toe a bit to help target it so you can focus your body awareness there. Feel its outline and shape with your bodily awareness. Move your body awareness back and forth through the big toe and continue this for one minute.

Shift your point of body awareness to your right knee, lightly rubbing or scratching it first to highlight it, and then repeat the above knee exercise. Then slowly move your point of body awareness down your leg and repeat the big toe exercise.

Repeat the above exercise with your left elbow joint and left thumb, and then your right elbow joint and right thumb.

Move your point of body awareness to several other parts of your body, anywhere you like, focusing on one part at a time. Feel your point of awareness moving over your body as you do this. Remember to feel each area as if trying to detect slight changes in air movement and air temperature there.

You have just moved your center of body awareness all around your body, targeting and focusing your body awareness in many parts. You also stimulated your energy body as your center of body awareness moved *through* your energy body. You may have felt some peculiar sensations. This is normal. Energy sensations will be discussed in more detail later.

Energy Work Demonstration

Now that you are familiar with the fundamental concepts, more hands-on practice will give you a better grasp of tactile imaging methods. It will also show you how to demonstrate tactile imaging to other people. One thing I have learned from teaching energy work to is that the easiest way to learn it is . . . to do energy work. The following exercises give you a better feel for your energy body and for running energy.

Key Points: Like the previous exercises, the key to effective energy work is to move your sense of *touch* and *feel* through your body. It helps if you feel that you are trying to sense tiny changes in air temperature and movement in the skin over the area you are focusing upon. Do not cross your legs when doing feet and leg exercises, as this increases difficulty. Cross your legs only after these methods have been mastered.

The strength and types of sensations caused by these exercises will vary from person to person. One side of your body will be more sensitive to energy movement than the other; for example, you may feel more energy in one hand or foot than the other. Which side this is will vary, depending upon your energetic makeup.

Again, eliminate distractions. Wear loose clothing, sit in a chair in a quiet place, and kick off your shoes. Place a cushion under your feet and do not cross your legs. Close your eyes and take a few deep breaths to settle yourself, and then start. Only light relaxation is required.

Combing Hair Exercise

Key Points: Your imaginary body awareness *hands* are the focal points for doing energy work. Ignore your arms. Your awareness hands are extensions of your body awareness. Imagine that your awareness arms will stretch to any length at any angle. Do not restrict your awareness hands to what your physical arms can do. In this way, you can reach any part of your body, even places you could not normally reach. Performing a body awareness action is like mentally rehearsing a physical action with imagination and body awareness feeling.

After you are relaxed and settled, with eyes closed, slowly raise your real physical hand and pretend to comb your hair with your fingers, brushing your fingers through your hair all over your head.

Focus your attention on what the movement of your hand feels like and on the touch of your fingertips moving over your head. *Remember* what these actions feel like so you can re-create them with body awareness alone. Take your time doing this.

Next, with arms resting in your lap or by your sides, slowly repeat the above actions *without* physically moving. Imagine and *feel* yourself slowly lifting your hand to your head. Focus on being aware of this action, of *imagining* and *feeling* it happening as if it really were. Focus on your imaginary fingers touching your head. Slowly comb your body awareness fingers through your hair, imagining and feeling this happening on your scalp. Continue this until you have combed the whole surface of your scalp and hair length several times.

Finish this exercise using both of your imaginary hands. Feel them slowly rising and then massaging your scalp, face, neck, and shoulders. Imagine and feel this happening slowly and in real time. Focus your attention on where your body awareness *hands* are touching you, and on feeling this contact in your body. Take your time over this.

Brushing Hands

With eyes open or shut, rest your left hand on your desk or lap, palm up, fingers together. With the fingertips of your right hand, stroke the whole surface of your left hand from wrist to fingertips repeatedly, taking about one second per stroke. Focus on what this feels like to your left hand. Memorize the feel of this touch. Continue stroking for 30 seconds, until you can reproduce the *feel* and *movement* of this touch in your left hand from memory alone and with your body awareness alone.

Stop physically stroking your hand and immediately continue moving the memory of the *feel* of the stroking action through the whole of your left hand, back and forth from fingertips to wrist. Continue this for a minute or more, until you have a good feeling for this action. Try it with eyes open and watching the action, and then with eyes shut.

You should begin to feel some vague peculiar sensations: a fuzziness, tightness, heaviness, pressure, tingling, or buzzing. The most common first sensation is a vague, fuzzy tightness or heaviness, like the residual feeling left behind after you have clapped your hands a few times. Any sensation, no mater how light or vague, indicates that some level of energy body stimulation is occurring. These sensations will be strong in some people, faint in others. The sensations will become more noticeable and consistent with practice. They may continue for some time even after you have stopped working on your hands. This is normal. Repeat the above exercise with your right hand.

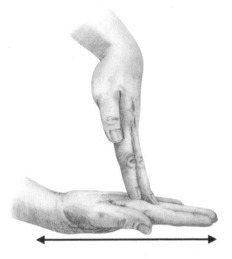

Repeat the above exercise with both hands simultaneously. Split body awareness actions are easy to do. Don't think about how to do it, just do this. First, rub your hands together and wiggle your fingers and make fists until you cause a slight, lasting physical sensation in them. Lay your hands palm up on your desk or lap. With eyes open or shut, focus on the sensation you caused, and then move the *feel* of this sensation back and forth from fingertips to wrists, through the whole of both hands simultaneously. Continue this for two minutes or more, until you have a good feeling for this action. You cannot overdo these exercises.

Brushing Feet Exercise

For the next exercise, first rub your bare feet on the floor or stamp them a little, and then wiggle your toes. This is to create a slight lasting sensation in your feet. Immediately place your feet on a cushion slightly out in front of you, and then close your eyes and feel for your feet with your sense of body awareness. Focus on your feet and feel with them as if you were trying to feel minute changes in air movement and air temperature there. When you are aware of where your feet are and how they feel, continue with the next step.

Perform the following exercise with your eyes closed. Start by brushing the underside of your left foot with your body awareness, moving the feel of the remembered sensation you caused in it back and forth. Brush back and forth from toes to heel, as if you were brushing the underside with a large paintbrush from underneath. When you can feel this action moving, let the feeling spread out so that you are *sponging* this feeling *through* the whole of your foot, from toes to heel. Take one or two seconds for either direction. Continue this for a few minutes or longer. Repeat the above exercise with your right foot.

Repeat the above exercise with both feet simultaneously. Rub your feet on the floor and wiggle your toes a little so you can feel your feet better. Next, put your feet together on a cushion slightly out in front of you. Brush the underside of both feet simultaneously, back and forth from toes to heels. When you can feel this action moving, let the feeling spread out so that you are sponging this feeling through the whole of both feet, from toes to heels simultaneously. Continue this for several minutes or longer. You cannot overdo hand and foot exercises.

Foot exercises can cause very strong, bone-deep tickling and tingling sensations in some people. If this gets too strong for comfort, stop and move on to the next exercise. Do this any time feet sensations get too strong, regardless of the instructions given.

Creating Energy Balls

An energy ball is a thought form construct. On the subtle energy level, this is real and not imaginary, and it will have a real effect upon your energy body.

Rub your hands together and wiggle your fingers and make fists to cause a slight, lasting sensation in them. Next, hold your hands out in front of your chest, cupping hands with fingers and thumbs almost touching, fingers slightly spread. Feel for the slight sensation you caused in your hands with your body awareness senses. Increase the intensity of this by feeling for minute changes of air movement and air temperature with your hands.

Close your eyes and imagine and feel that an electric blue, tennis

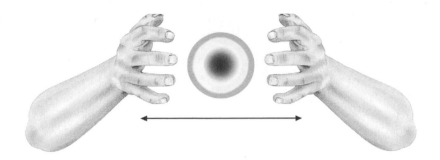

ball–sized energy ball is forming between your hands. Imagine and feel this energy ball spinning between your hands. You may not actually see this, but you can imagine and feel this. Continue this for a minute or two.

Slowly move your hands 12 inches or so apart. Imagine and feel the energy ball staying put and hovering in space between your hands. Next, imagine and feel the energy ball moving so it bounces from hand to hand. Feel the ball touching each hand as strongly as you can. Imagine, feel, and sense this happening. Then imagine and feel that the ball is passing through and several inches past each hand. Play with the ball until you get a feel for this, speeding it up and slowing it down. Continue for two minutes or longer.

Hug Circuit

With eyes open or shut, hold your hands together with fingers linked out in front of you as if you were hugging a tree. Focus on your hands and feel them with your body awareness senses. Imagine an electric blue energy ball forming over your hands where your fingers are linked, slightly larger than before. Imagine and feel the energy ball moving easily through your flesh. Move it up your right wrist and arm to your shoulder, and then through your chest and heart and out your left shoulder, and then down your arm and back to your hands. Keep the energy ball moving and repeat this, moving the energy ball around and around through your arms and chest. Each circuit should take about two to four seconds. Experiment with the speed and use what works best for you. Continue for two minutes or so.

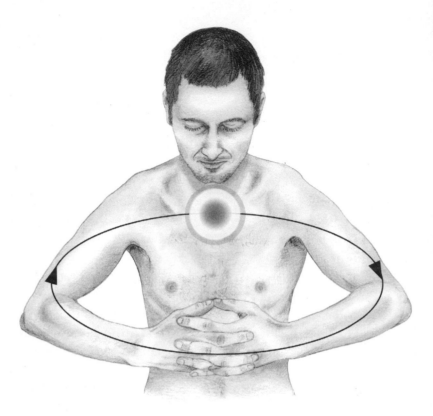

Brow Brushing and Wrapping

Rub or lightly scratch the middle of your forehead to help target your brow. Close your eyes and focus on the residual sensation you caused there with your body awareness senses. Then brush the whole of your brow from temple to temple for one minute as if you were brushing that area with a paint brush. Feel this brushing action moving across your brow.

Extend the brushing action and move it all the way around your head at brow level, around and around. Direction is unimportant. Brush around your head as if you were wrapping a bandage around your head. Continue for two minutes or more.

Brow Center Bounce

Rub or scratch the middle of your forehead again to help with targeting. Imagine and feel an electric blue energy ball forming there, one about the size of a golf ball. Imagine and feel this energy ball moving into and through your head to a few inches out of the back of your head at the same level. Then bring it back through your head to a few inches in front of your brow. Start bouncing the energy ball back and forth through your head, feeling it passing through your brain. Continue for two minutes or more.

Temple Bounce

Rub or lightly scratch your left and right temples. Focus your body awareness in your right temple and imagine a small golf ball–sized, electric blue energy ball forming there. Move the ball through your head and brain and out of your left temple, a few inches outside. Then move it back through your head and brain to a few inches out past your right temple. Feel the energy ball passing through the substance of your brain. Bounce the energy ball back and forth through your brain, about one-half to one second each way. Continue for two minutes or more.

As you have discovered, tactile imaging is an easy and effective way to stimulate your energy body. The type and intensity of sensations caused by these exercises will vary from person to person. Most people will feel at least some noticeable sensations from these exercises. Some people will feel a lot more.

Note: The exercises you have just done can activate the heart center and/or the brow center in some people. Do not be surprised if you feel tingling and/or light throbbing in your heart or brow areas, or even a mild tightness in your chest and tingling in your spine. These are normal sensations for this type of energy body stimulation.

Sensing Hand Energy

This exercise shows you how to sense and feel human energy fields, starting with your own. Relax and hold your hands 12 inches apart and focus your body awareness senses in your hands. Feel them as intensely as you can, as if trying to feel minute changes in air movement and air temperature. Move your hands slowly together until they are almost touching, and then move them apart again. Do this slowly, over and over, while feeling and sensing with your hands. You will feel a slight resistance, a slight texture and pressure, as your hands move closer together. The distance this pressure can be felt at varies from person to person. Continue for as long as you like.

Two Person Exercise

The energy of another person can be easier to sense than your own. Find a partner and instruct them on how to feel energy. Then do the following: stand facing about six feet (two meters) apart. Hold up your hands so your palms are facing the palms of the other person. Both of you focus body awareness in your hands, and feel and sense with them as strongly as you can. Both of you move your hands slowly closer to each other's hands until you are almost touching. Move your hands very slowly in and out, both of you sensing and trying to detect the energy field of the other's hands. Step back a few paces, and then step in closer, sensing all the time. Again, imagine you are trying to detect tiny changes in air movement and air temperature. At certain points you will feel faint textures and delicate pressures in your hands as your hands react to your partner's subtle energy fields. Continue this as long as you like.

If you have felt nothing at all so far, please repeat the exercises given earlier until you feel some sensations. If you still feel nothing after doing this, move on to the next section. It is rare to feel nothing, but sometimes it takes a little time before energy sensations are perceived.

Next, we will build on tactile imaging with some simple but effective methods for relaxing the body and quieting the mind.

Physical Relaxation

The effectiveness of energy work can be improved by relaxing and balancing your physical body at the start of each session. The simplest way to achieve this is to tense and relax large groups of muscles. After each step below, when you release and relax, take a few moments to imagine and feel the tension flowing out of your body.

1. Sit and close your eyes, and then take three slow deep breaths.
2. Tense your feet and legs, and then release and relax them.

3. Tense your hips and stomach area, and then release and relax them.
4. Tense your chest and arms, making fists, and then release and relax them.
5. Tense your head and face and neck, and then release and relax them.
6. Tense your whole body, and then release and relax it.

When you finish the last step above, feel yourself going limp and sinking into your chair. Imagine and feel all of the tension draining down your body and out of your feet like imaginary discolored fluid. Feel and imagine this draining away and soaking away into the ground. Next, resettle yourself in the chair so that you are comfortable and balanced. Pay particular attention to balancing your head.

Note: People—especially women—tend to hold tension in their stomach area. It is wise to make a conscious effort to relax this area.

Awareness Belly Breathing

The stomach area contains the largest primary energy center in your body, the navel center. The stomach and the breathing process can be used to help quiet and relax your mind. The body awareness belly breathing method given here is the simplest way I have found to achieve this.

Awareness belly breathing can be done anytime, anywhere. Waiting and travel time are excellent opportunities for practicing mental relaxation and energy work. Belly breathing promotes deep physical and mental relaxation. A relaxed state provides a clearer inner focus. It also increases energy body sensitivity and its responses to stimulation actions.

Awareness belly breathing involves focusing your body awareness on the physical sensation of breathing, on the rise and fall of your stomach. Sit quietly, close your eyes, and focus your attention on your stomach. Take your time and try to become more aware of this area. Let your stomach sag and relax. Breathe a little more deeply from your stomach, feeling it rising and falling as you breathe. Observe this action and use this focus of attention to help clear and relax your mind. Hold your mind clear of thought words. If thought words begin, simply release them and bring your attention back to your breathing and stomach movement. No matter how many times distracting thoughts creep in, just push them away and refocus on your stomach. This takes a little practice, but it is the easiest method I have found for relaxing the mind.

Altered States of Consciousness

A combination of physical relaxation and belly breathing will help you achieve altered states of consciousness. There are many conscious-altered state levels possible, and these are related to the levels of sleep. When you slip into an altered state, you will feel a warm, cozy, and heavy wave pass over your body. This is a perfectly natural state. It happens every time you start falling asleep.

You can experience an altered state by observing yourself while falling asleep. To do this, lie on your back and hold your forearms vertical with elbows resting on the bed. Let yourself drift towards sleep while observing what is happening. (Awareness belly breathing will help this process.) When you start drifting off, your arms will drop and jerk you awake. Repeat this process many times and you will experience the altered state of consciousness involved with falling asleep. This may be only for a few moments, but it is valuable first-hand experience. You will then know what an altered state of consciousness feels like.

It is common for people to appear to fall asleep during relaxation and meditation exercises. You may at times hear yourself snoring or making sleep sounds, even though your mind is still fully awake and aware. This is because of the relationship between altered states and sleep. In an altered state of consciousness, your mind stays awake while your body is asleep. Falling too deeply asleep will cause loss of consciousness, which needs to be avoided for effective altered state energy work. This can be overcome by using a hard-backed chair with no head support. This will help to keep the mind/body connection alive, which is necessary to function in an altered state.

Calming the Mind

For most people, quieting the mind is not easy. This goes against a lifetime of unfettered, spontaneous thinking and free-flowing mental association. Thought words are the biggest problem, followed by emotionally charged mental imagery. Awareness belly breathing will help focus your mind, but thought words will keep trying to creep in and get your attention. This is like having an annoying message and reminder service. It reacts impulsively, stating and restating the obvious, making inane comments, jokes, et cetera. This serves a purpose in life in the fully awake state and generally goes unnoticed. It only becomes a problem when you are trying to relax and quiet your mind.

To calm your mind enough to induce an altered state of consciousness takes practice. Thought word reminders and worries will keep trying to get your attention. This is distracting when you are trying to focus your mind, to meditate, and to do inner work. Apart from awareness belly breathing, there are a couple of things you can do to reduce the mental pressure. The first is to make a simple affirmation, ordering your mind to be quiet. For example, when your mind starts chattering or imagining, firmly state the following command in your mind: "I choose not to think about that. I choose to relax and clear my mind." Restate this every time you are distracted by thought words. These can be rephrased to be more specific; for example, "I choose not to think about money. I choose to think of nothing."

Another way of reducing the pressure of thoughts and worries is journaling. Before your relaxation or energy work session, take pen and paper and for ten minutes or so write down anything that is bothering you. Just write down the first thing that pops into your head, including random thoughts, and continue from there. This works because you are taking action on your thoughts and worries and recording them in a concrete way. This reduces the thought pressure from within that is trying to bring these things to your attention and have them dealt with. These methods also help insomnia, if caused by worrisome thoughts.

Practice

Loosen clothing, sit in a chair with shoes off and feet on a cushion, take a few deep breaths, and begin. Stretch and relax large muscle groups of your body, as explained earlier. Close your eyes and focus on your belly, letting it relax and sag. Start awareness belly breathing. Feel your stomach rising and falling as you breathe in and out. Keep your mind clear and focus solely on your breathing. When you are settled into this, begin to imagine a sinking feeling. Imagine that you and your chair are in an elevator that is slowly descending into an open-sided elevator shaft. Imagine that you can see the rock walls of the elevator shaft rising as you move deeper and deeper and deeper. Continue this for 15 minutes or longer.

These physical and mental relaxation methods will be used extensively in the rest of this book.

THREE

Running Energy

As said earlier, the best way to learn energy work is by doing energy work. This chapter teaches a variety of techniques for stimulating different parts of the energy body, for storing energy, and for running energy circuits. Perform each of the coming exercises in the order they are presented.

If you feel nothing after doing any of these exercises for several minutes, move to the next. While energy movement sensations are apparent in the majority of cases, some may feel little in the early stages. A complete lack of sensation is rare. No sensations at all after several energy work sessions usually indicates that the energy body is blocked or inactive in the areas being worked upon. If this is the case, continue with these exercises as best you can. Energy work exercises given later in this book are designed to help restore stubborn, inactive areas and remove blockages. A hot shower or bath sensitizes the physical body to energy movement sensations and promotes stronger general energy flow. Taking a cool shower and scrubbing your body with a soft brush will help even more. Try this if you have trouble feeling energy movement.

When a repetitive body awareness action is done, it soon gains momentum. It will often continue on its own even after you stop consciously performing the action. This natural phenomenon makes energy work easier to do. However, it can cause your focal point of body awareness to become locked into a specific area or into a particular action. This can be helpful if you are performing a self-healing action and want it to continue after falling asleep, but it can be annoying if you want to work on other areas. If this happens, try switching to brushing your hands and feet until the problem eases.

Tactile Imaging Techniques

The tactile imaging techniques coming up are used in a variety of ways for stimulating your energy body and energy centers throughout this book. In doing all these exercises, remember the golden rule of energy work: If energy sensations become overly strong, painful, or worrying, cease all energy work. Rest and ground yourself until all worrying sensations are gone. Then return to energy work and continue a little more gently. It is wise to follow this rule, as it avoids most potential problems.

Energy Balls

Energy balls, introduced earlier, will be used a lot in the work ahead. Just imagine a ball of energy forming and moving, as we did earlier. Energy balls can be moved through the body, around the body, and even outside of the body. An energy ball can be expanded and contracted or exploded and shrunk. This can be done to provide stronger stimulation in a particular area or to shake up and wear away an energy blockage.

Energy balls can also be combined with a sponging action. This is a whole-of-limb action, mainly used for raising energy. This is also used for energy bounce actions, which will be introduced shortly. To perform an energy ball sponging action, imagine and feel that you are pulling a large wet sponge ball through a limb. Feel it moving through its whole substance, muscles and bones.

Brushing and Stirring Actions

Brushing and stirring actions have a variety of uses. For example, the exercise we did earlier, where you brushed your hands and feet, used a brushing action. The stirring action is used mainly for direct stimulation of primary energy centers, large secondary centers, and for deeper stimulation of energy exchange areas.

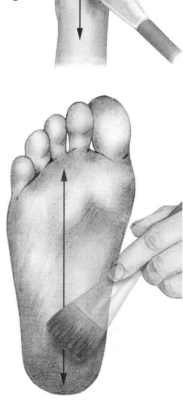

Wrapping Action

The wrapping action is used for stimulating larger areas; for example, wrapping a finger, forearm, or leg. This is also an excellent self-healing action that can be used both on the surface of and inside the body.

Tearing Action

The tearing action is mainly used for stimulating primary energy centers, although it can be used to stimulate smaller areas. Imagine and feel that you are tearing apart a doughnut or bread roll about the size of your fist with a two-handed action. Repeat this action over and over.

Energy Center Breathing

This action is mainly used on primary energy centers. Start by focusing your awareness in your base center, in the perineum (flat area between the anus and genitals). Start breathing *in* and feel yourself breathing into your base center, and then feel yourself breathing *out* through your base center. Continue for several breaths or more, and then move on to your navel center, solar plexus, heart, throat, brow, and crown.

Body Awareness Bounce Actions

The energy bounce, also introduced earlier, is effective for stimulat-

ing any part of your body. To bounce energy, move your body awareness back and forth through a body part, say the spine, as if you were
bouncing a ball of energy there. The speed of a bounce action is set
by your ability to stay in touch with the feeling the action produces in
your physical body. If the
bounce is too slow, stimulation is reduced. If it is too
fast, you will lose body
awareness contact and the
action becomes ineffective.
When doing a bounce
action, speed up the action
until you start to lose touch,
and then slow it down until
a comfortable bounce speed
with full body awareness
contact and feel is achieved.

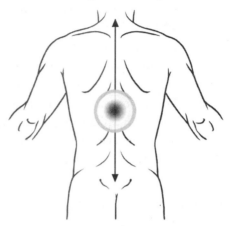

Hand and Foot Work

The hands and feet are crucial areas to stimulate for energy work. This
cannot be emphasized enough. Consider the importance of the hands
and feet in acupuncture and reflexology, and how working on these areas
profoundly affects the functioning and health of the entire body.

Apart from breathing, the hands and feet are the main portals of
subtle energy into your body. Imagine these as being like the vital
roots and leaves of a tree. Energy cannot be raised or projected effectively until the hands and feet become sensitized and conditioned to
a higher flow of subtle energy.

If you have not done energy work before, you'll find that most of
the finer structures of your energy body will be dormant. This
includes the hands and feet and primary energy centers. They are
dormant because they have never really been used at levels exceeding
the demands of normal physical life. Energy work will change this
fairly quickly. You will find the process of waking up the structures of
your energy body to be a fascinating experience.

Again, most people will find that one side of the body is more sensitive to energy work than the other. Which side this is varies. Spend more time on inactive areas and less time on more sensitive areas to help balance energy body development.

The following processes involve some fine energy work on the hands and feet. This is necessary to clear and activate small energy centers and connecting pathways, and to clear and sensitize groups of energy exchange pores. This may seem laborious, but it is well worth the effort. Please carry out the following exercises thoroughly.

Key Point: Focusing your body awareness keenly in the area you are working upon will help with these exercises. Again, feel with your body as if you are trying to detect tiny changes in air temperature and air movement upon the area you are working.

Hand and Arm Work

The following exercises are normally done during training, where the energy body is being sensitized to body awareness actions. However, these should be repeated periodically, say once a month, to keep these areas clear and active. Pay more attention to areas where energy work causes the least physical sensations.

Finger Energy Balls

Sitting comfortably, lay your left hand on your lap, cushion, or desk, with the palm down and the fingers slightly spread. Look at your hand. Brush the whole of your hand from fingertips to wrist, as we did in the demonstration exercise, for a minute or so. Follow this action up and down with your eyes.

Next, focus on your left thumb. Wiggle this and give it a rub to help target it with body awareness. Imagine and feel a small, electric blue ball of energy hovering over the tip of your thumb. Its diameter should be slightly larger than your thumb. Feel and imagine this ball of energy moving from the tip of your thumb, down through the thumb bone, and past the big joint at your wrist. Move this back and forth through your thumb repeatedly with a bounce action. Take about one-half second or less in each direction, but vary the speed to suit yourself. It is important to maintain body awareness contact with your thumb and to feel this movement in your thumb. Continue this for 30 seconds or more.

Repeat the above exercise on each of the fingers of your left hand. Repeat the above exercise on the thumb and fingers of your right hand. Finally, turn your hands over so they are face up, one hand at a time, and repeat the above exercise on the fingers and thumbs of both hands.

Palm Work

Lay your left hand on your lap, a desk, or a cushion, palm up. Flex your fingers a few times, make a fist, and rub or lightly scratch the middle of your palm to highlight it with body awareness. Use a small, brisk body awareness stirring action, about an inch across, to stir the middle of your palm. Continue for 30 seconds or so, and then move this rotary action over the palm and underside of the fingers of your hand. Work your way over the entire surface area, taking your time. Continue this for several minutes, until you have covered the entire underside of your hand from fingertips to wrist several times. Stir in whichever direction feels best.

Repeat the above exercise with your right hand.

Arm Wrapping

Lean to your left a little and let your left arm hang comfortably by your side, but not touching your side. Use a wide body awareness

wrapping action, as if covering your arm with a four-inch overlapping bandage. Work your way up your arm to your shoulder and then back down to your fingertips. Pay extra attention to your wrist, elbow, and shoulder joints. Continue this for two minutes or longer.

Perform the above exercise with your right hand and arm.

Arm Energy Balls

Flex your left hand and arm, wiggling your fingers and making a fist a few times to help focus body awareness. Let your arm hang comfortably by your side again. Imagine and feel an energy ball forming over your hand. Move the energy ball from your fingertips to your shoulder and then back to fingertips, bouncing up and down repeatedly. Take about one-half to one second either way. Feel this action moving through the whole of your hand and arm as the energy ball moves through your flesh and bone. Continue for two minutes or longer. Vary the bounce speed, slowing down and speeding up to find what has the most effect on you.

Perform the above exercise on your right arm. Then perform the above exercise on both arms simultaneously.

Footwork

To prepare, remove your shoes and sit in a chair with your heels resting comfortably on a cushion, legs slightly apart and out in front. Do not cross your legs and do not have your feet flat on the floor, as this will make these exercises more difficult. If you have difficulty feeling your feet with body awareness, wash, soak, and scrub them in warm water and/or take a hot shower beforehand. Look at your feet and follow the body awareness actions with your eyes, as this will help you target individual toes better.

Note: A very small percentage of people have feet that are so sensitive that energy work on the feet is too uncomfortable to perform. If this is the case, just do the best you can. Avoid strong footwork if it is too uncomfortable. Simply focusing on your feet as if you are trying to detect small changes in air temperature and movement should provide ample stimulation.

Toe Work

The smaller toes are more difficult to focus on with body awareness, but this is still doable. Scratch, rub, and wiggle your toes as needed to help target them. When you work on the smallest toe, move the energy ball back and forth down the side of your foot from small toe to side of heel. This action can produce strong sensations.

To begin, first use a brushing action across all of the toes of your left foot, from side to side. Feel this deep inside all of your toes. Continue this for a minute or longer.

Focus body awareness in your left big toe. Wiggle, rub, or scratch it to help target this area. Feel and imagine an energy ball forming over the tip of your big toe. Move this energy ball down through your big toe and to the ball of your foot. Feel this as keenly as you can with body awareness. Move the energy ball back and forth repeatedly, bouncing it from the tip of your big toe to the ball of your foot. Continue for two minutes or until you feel your big toe respond with noticeable energy sensations. Once a toe responds, move on to the next.

Repeat the above exercise on each toe of your left foot. Then perform the above exercises on each of the toes of your right foot.

Sole Work

This exercise is similar to the rotary stirring action we did earlier on the undersides of the hands. Wiggle your toes and rub them on the floor as necessary to help focus body awareness in the ball of your left foot. Focus on this area and use a rotary stirring action about one inch across. Feel this stirring action deep inside your flesh and bone. Continue stirring and move this rotary action slowly and thoroughly over the whole underside of your foot, including the undersides of your toes and heels. Continue for two minutes or more.

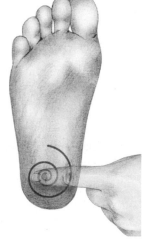

Perform the above exercise on your right foot.

Heel and Ankle Work

Focus body awareness in your left heel. Feel and imagine an energy ball forming there about the size of your heel. Using a bounce action, move the energy ball up your leg to just above your ankle, and then back to heel repeatedly. Then use a stirring action on your heel. Finish with a rapidly expanding and contracting energy ball in your heel.

Move an energy ball side to side through your ankle repeatedly. Then move the ball back and forth through your ankle repeatedly. Then use an expanding and contracting energy ball in your ankle joint. Finish with a wrapping action around your ankle, as if applying a bandage. Repeat the above actions on your right foot.

With your feet side by side and several inches apart, bounce an energy ball from ankle to ankle, passing through each ankle and slightly outside your body on each side. Continue for a minute or more.

Two Foot Ankle Circuit

This exercise stimulates the feet and helps remove blockages, which are common in feet. Place your feet side by side. Create energy balls, one for each foot. Move them through your feet simultaneously, from toes to heels, and then up through your ankles and out over the top of your feet to your toes again, repeatedly. Continue for a minute or two. Reverse the direction and continue for another minute or two.

More Hand and Footwork

After the detailed hand and foot exercises have been accomplished thoroughly, the following exercises should be repeated periodically to keep hands and feet clear and active. Other than from doing this work, the hands and the feet are normally stimulated with larger dual body awareness actions. For example, the feet are stimulated with two energy balls, one for each foot. These are moved simultaneously back and fourth through your feet. The hands are stimulated in the same way. These actions must be felt through the whole of the area you are working upon, deep inside your flesh and bones, as if sponging the energy balls through your body. Spend more time working on inactive areas to clear blockages.

Every toe and finger joint can be worked upon with brushing and stirring and wrapping actions: top, bottom, and sides. The legs and arms can also be worked upon in the same way. This process takes longer to do, but the extra attention will help clear and condition these important energy body conduits.

Leg and Knee Work

Flex and tense your left foot and leg, wiggling the toes and foot, to help focus body awareness there. Hold your leg reasonably straight. Imagine and feel an energy ball forming over your foot large enough to fit over your thigh. Using a bounce action, move the energy ball from your foot up to your hip joint and then back to your foot, repeatedly. Take about one-half to one second either way. Feel this action moving through the whole of your leg as the energy ball moves through your flesh and bones. Continue for a few minutes or longer. Vary the speed, slowing down and speeding up to find what produces the strongest sensations in your leg.

Repeat the above exercise on your right leg. Then perform the above exercise on both legs simultaneously.

Focus body awareness in your left knee. Use the stirring action on the kneecap. Form an energy ball and work this through the knee joint, back and forth and then side to side. Then use an expanding and contracting energy ball in the knee. Then use an exploding and contracting energy ball in the knee. Hold your knees several inches apart and bounce an energy ball from knee to knee. Finish by using a wrapping action around your knee.

Repeat the above exercises on your right knee.

Leg Energy Raising

For primary center work, you will need to be able to raise or *sweep* energy up your legs. This is much like a sponging energy ball leg bounce action, but without the downward stroke. Form energy balls in your feet and move these up your legs to your hips while imagining and feeling that you are sweeping, sponging, and pulling something like water up your legs. Then flick your awareness back to your feet and repeat the upward energy sweep over and over.

Whole Body Bounce

The whole body bounce stimulates the entire body. Imagine and feel a large, electric blue energy ball that is large enough to pass over your whole body forming over your feet. Move the ball up your legs and torso to just above your head, and then back down to just below your feet. Adjust the speed of this until you have a comfortable bounce action. Continue this for two minutes or longer.

Note: An alternative to an energy ball is to use a large flat disk for whole body bounce actions. Do what works best for you.

Pre-Stimulation

The pre-stimulation exercise prepares your energy body for an energy work session. The idea is to give a quick boost to energy body activity and sensitivity. This can be done quickly and easily. This should be done prior to any energy work session. To pre-stimulate, spend several seconds stimulating your feet, then your legs, then your hands, and then your arms. Finally, use a whole body bounce action for a minute or so.

Energy Circuits

An energy circuit is a body awareness action that moves in a continuous loop, utilizing the energy momentum factor. Breathing is often used to enhance this type of action. Energy circuits have two main purposes: to cause widespread stimulation and to accumulate and store energy.

With energy raising exercises, it can help if you imagine and feel as if you are sweeping up water through your body. For example, with leg exercises, imagine and feel yourself holding a large sponge ball and sponging water upwards through the *whole* of your legs. Imagine that the water keeps trying to run back down your leg and that body awareness and imagination effort are needed to force the water to rise. This helps give body awareness actions something to grip onto, increasing the effectiveness of energy raising actions.

Full Body Circuit

The following exercise moves energy around your body and into your sub-navel storage center. This action—combined with the intention to move and store energy—causes widespread energy body stimulation and a flow of energy. This can be done in any position; for example, sitting, standing, or lying down. It is best done with your arms by your sides.

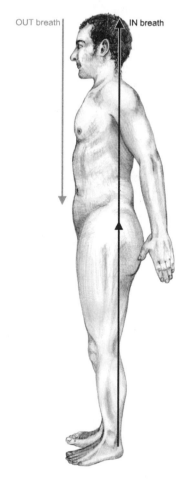

Pre-stimulate the hands and arms, and feet and legs, and then use a whole body bounce for a minute or so. Focus body awareness in your feet and as you breathe *in* move your body awareness up through your legs and through your back and neck to the top of your head. Hold your awareness there and as you finish the *in* breath. As you start to breathe *out*, move your body awareness down through your face and neck, and down over your chest. Feel it flowing into your sub-navel storage center as you complete the *out* breath. Switch your focus back to your feet and repeat. Continue for several minutes or for as long as necessary.

On the *in* breath, as you raise energy past where your hands and arms are resting, try to include these loosely in the upwards energy raising action. The target area for energy storage is your sub-navel area.

The full body circuit action does not have to be precise. Feel your energy widening out as it moves up and over your back, loosely including your arms and up to the top of your head. As you move body awareness down, just generally feel it moving through your face, mouth, and neck, and then spreading out as it moves over and through your chest and stomach. Then push this energy feeling into your lower stomach area while you finish the *out* breath. Then switch back to your feet and repeat as you start the next *in* breath. This circuit can be continued for as long as desired. It also helps occupy and calm the mind, as this has similarities with awareness belly breathing.

Breathing Storage and Healing Circuit

Pre-stimulate. Lay your hands on your sub-navel center. Focus body awareness in your feet. As you breathe *in,* raise energy up through your legs and torso and to your heart center. Hold your awareness in your heart and feel your energy accumulating there until you finish the *in* breath. As you start breathing *out*, move your energy out through your shoulders and arms and hands and into your sub-navel storage center. Continue for as long as desired.

The breathing circuit is similar to the heart center healing method given later in this book. The only difference here is that your energy and intention are directed to store energy in your sub-navel center rather than to project energy. This circuit also helps relax and calm the mind.

The breathing circuit can also be used to self-heal specific parts of your body; for example, by placing your hands on a damaged or diseased area to give healing there.

Standing Energy Storage Practice

Energy storage can be enhanced with the following practice: Pre-stimulate and stand with your legs slightly apart and your arms hanging slightly out from your sides, palms forward and with fingers spread. As you breathe *in*, raise energy from your feet to your heart center, as we did earlier. As you breathe *out*, breathe the energy out through your arms and hands. As you do this, move your arms out wide and low before you, and imagine that you are physically scooping a cloud of energy into your lower stomach area with your hands. Feel the energy flowing through your arms into your lower stomach, into your sub-navel center, as you complete the *out* breath.

Finish this action with your hands resting on your lower stomach. Repeat this action several times, or as desired. It cannot be overdone.

The power of this practice can be increased by facing the sunrise or sunset, the ocean, a lake or river, waterfall or mountains, or any beautiful natural setting. Stormy weather greatly increases the available energy in the atmosphere. This is a good time to raise and absorb extra energy and for self-healing practice.

Simple Body Awareness Breathing

This exercise stimulates the whole energy body in a very simple way, using breathing to regulate a gentle whole body bounce action. This is also good for relaxing and calming the mind.

Pre-stimulate. Focus your awareness in your feet. As you breathe *in*, move your awareness up your legs and up through your whole body to your head, loosely including awareness of your arms. As you breathe *out*, move your awareness back down through your body to your feet. Synchronize the up and down action with your breathing. Continue for as long as desired.

Another version of this exercise is to focus awareness on your perineum (flat area between the anus and genitals). As you breathe *in*, take your awareness up through your central channel to your crown center. As you breathe *out*, move your awareness back down through your central channel to your perineum. Repeat the up and down action with each breath. Continue for as long as desired.

Many energy circuits are possible, involving the whole body or its parts. Experiment and make up some of your own. What works, works. This can be helpful for treating energy blockages in specific parts of your body.

Energy Movement Sensations

Energy movement causes some unusual sensations, which vary in intensity from person to person. The most common include tingling, buzzing, fluttering, throbbing, body hair prickling, mild cramping or tightness, heaviness, fuzziness, bone-deep tickling, and warm or cool sensations.

A number of things contribute to energy movement sensations: physical body nerve sensitivity, physical body damage and disease, and energy body resistance. Typically, resistance to energy flow is caused by sluggish or stuck energy, and by energy blockages.

Strong energy movement sensations *always* reduce as your energy body becomes sensitized to improved energy flow, as energy blockages are cleared, and as your energy body develops. It is a natural mistake to think that you might be doing something wrong, when once strong energy sensations reduce with continued practice. The opposite applies here.

Very few people will feel little or nothing, even in the early demonstration exercises. Most will experience noticeable sensations. But a minority of people will feel *overly* strong sensations to the point where it may be too uncomfortable to continue some exercises at that time. Hypersensitivity to energy movement usually occurs in the feet and hands. These are typically comprised of intense bone-deep buzzing, tingling, and tickling sensations similar to how your leg feels when it goes to sleep and you try to move it too soon. If this is the case, spend less time on feet or hand exercises until such time as the discomfort reduces.

I have taught these methods for many years, and in that time, I have only encountered a small group of people who have energy work hypersensitivity. A few people have even fallen off their chairs and been unable to stand for several minutes due to major sensations caused by early work. In all cases, this has involved the feet and legs. However, most of these people found that the hypersensitivity reduced rapidly, and within a few days they were able to perform normal energy work on their feet and legs.

Falling asleep is usually not a problem during energy work sessions because the work promotes mental alertness. Because of this, doing too much energy work directly before bed can make falling asleep difficult. This affects some people more than others. Keep this in mind if you find it hard to fall asleep after energy work sessions. Reduce time spent energy working before sleep accordingly. The best remedy I have found for this is a late night snack.

Caution: You will progress more rapidly with body awareness energy work than you will with other energetic systems. This is because body awareness actions have a more direct impact upon the energy body. This results in more rapid energy body development.

Remember the Golden Rule: If energy sensations become too strong or worrisome for you, stop all energy work and take a break until you feel normal again. Then return to energy work a little more gently.

Practice

Carry out the physical relaxation exercise, and then pre-stimulate your hands and feet with energy balls and do awareness belly breathing for a few minutes—until you are nice and relaxed. Use bounce actions on your legs and then your arms. Then do a spinal bounce followed by a whole body bounce. Perform the full body circuit for a few minutes, and then do the breathing circuit for a few minutes. Then return to awareness belly breathing and spend at least 15 minutes, relaxing and quieting your mind and deepening your level of relaxation.

The energy work you have done so far has mainly involved secondary and tertiary structures. It is important to be comfortable with these levels of energy work before approaching the primary energy centers.

FOUR

Primary Energy Center Work

This chapter's goal is to impart a workable understanding of primary energy centers and structures to help you to practice stimulating primary centers.

Primary energy centers are the major subtle organs of the energy body. They connect into the spine, major organs, glands, and ganglia of the human body. They are also interconnected through the spine and the central channel, and in that sense, they form a single, column-like energetic structure. Individually, primary centers generate vortexes of energy that can be seen clairvoyantly as spinning wheels of subtle light on the surface of the physical body. These are most visible when observed from the front and less visible to the rear.

Primary centers are smaller when dormant. They increase in size as they develop. They are always active on some level, even when spiritually dormant because they are intimately related to the act of living. Noticeable activity does not usually occur unless they are energetically stimulated in some way, which triggers higher activity and functions. (This can also happen spontaneously.) Increased activity produces a variety of physical sensations and spiritual phenomena. They begin to grow and develop when regularly stimulated by spiritual practice, and those doing this type of work also begin to evolve spiritually and psychically.

The true nature of primary energy centers is complex. Expounding upon their mysteries often becomes an exercise in mythical analogy and spiritual poetry. This can be confusing to the Western mind. To overcome this, I focus on two of the major functions of primary centers: the transformation and accumulation of subtle energies.

Following is a practical description of primary energy center structures and some of the sensations they produce when activated.

The Base Center Structure

The base primary center is centered in the perineum. This is part of a large energy structure occupying the pelvic area. It is composed of five powerful energy centers: the perineum, genitals, coccyx, and both hip joints. The perineum center joins this structure to the lower end of the central channel. A large amount of energy flows up through the legs and feeds into either side of the base structure. Stimulating any part of this structure will contribute to the activity of the base center as a whole. Each of these centers can produce strong sensations when directly stimulated.

The following illustrations show a cross section and a frontal view of the base center structure, showing the five major energy centers involved. Extending down through the middle of the torso is the central channel. This is like a tube of force that extends through the full length of the torso and head of the physical body. This is centered over the perineum area of the base center structure.

The base center is the most important center to stimulate for energy body development. The higher primary centers, especially

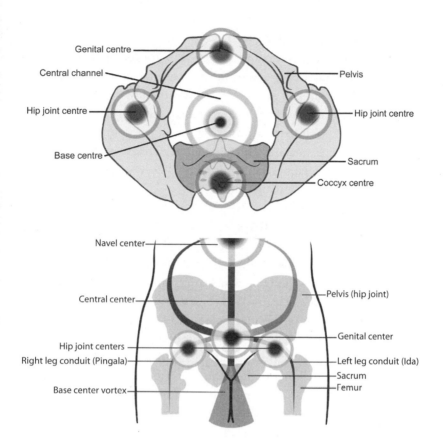

the brow and crown centers, should not be overworked until the base primary center is sufficiently developed, as this can cause imbalance. However, an apparently inactive base center will not stop higher primary centers from functioning. All primary centers can function independently. For example, while your base primary center may appear unresponsive, your solar plexus primary center may be naturally active. The sensitivity and potential activity or inactivity of individual primary centers varies greatly from person to person.

The best approach to primary center development is to nurture the energy body as a whole structure. This promotes healthy energetic balance and spiritual development. In order to accomplish this, inactive primary centers require more attention than others.

Base Structure—Perineum

The main energy vortex of the base primary center flowers in the perineum, the flat area between the anus and genitals. This position may seem like a difficult area to focus on with body awareness, but in practice, this is quite easy to do. When active, the perineum will throb and tingle noticeably. Sensations of tightness, cramping, and heat are also common, particularly during and after early stimulation sessions. A residual feeling of mild bruising, like what comes from riding a bike for a long time, is common.

Base Structure—Genitals

This vortex center covers the genital area, male or female. Direct body awareness actions on this center will cause strong erotic stimulation. This can cause problems during energy work sessions, for obvious reasons. It is best to avoid this center entirely. Do not worry if you occasionally feel mild erotic sensations there, even when this area has not been stimulated directly. Because of the base center's proximity to the genital area, body awareness actions sometimes intrude and cause erotic stimulation. Move on to another exercise and this usually will not cause any lasting problems. If body awareness becomes locked into this area and this causes a problem, heavy exercise and a cold shower are recommended to deactivate this center.

Sexual Energy and Lovemaking

Sex and sexuality are massively related energetically. These are essential ingredients of life and health. Sexual problems can be devastating and, therefore, deserve as much attention as any other healing-related issue. This idea of using body awareness energy work methods for erotic stimulation and lovemaking came to me in the mid-1990s. I was presented with a number of healing cases involving couples with sexual problems; for example, low libido, frigidity, impotence, et cetera. I soon began receiving letters saying, "You have saved our marriage!" The results were so successful that I have recommended and fine-tuned these ideas ever since. I have received only positive feedback concerning the use of body awareness energy work to enhance lovemaking. Sex and sexuality are such important aspects of life and health that I think everyone needs to know how this works.

The genital energy center is the most naturally active of all energy centers. For the majority of people, this powerhouse of energy provides the only significant energy-related sensations ever experienced. A massive amount of sexual energy is produced and exchanged during lovemaking. The practice of body awareness energy work puts you in touch with your energy body, which in turn puts you more closely in touch with your physical body. In time, this reveals new levels of awareness: physical body awareness, emotional sensitivity, sexuality, and intimacy.

Body awareness actions, when performed directly on the genital area, will cause intense erotic stimulation. If continued, this will lead to unusually powerful orgasms, even where no actual physical stimulation is involved. While obviously distracting and best avoided during energy work and spiritual practices, this factor can be used to augment lovemaking. The brushing, stirring, wrapping, bouncing, and energy ball methods given earlier can all be adapted for erotic stimulation. These can be applied both internally and externally.

Body awareness actions can be shifted outside of your own body to stimulate the energy body of another person, again both internally and externally. In this way, two people working together can significantly enhance the intensity of their lovemaking by stimulating their own and each other's genital centers and erogenous zones simultaneously.

The hands, mouth, genitals—indeed any part of the body—can be used in varied imaginative ways to project and receive erotic stimulation. The hands, for example, can be charged with sexual energy by sensing with them, as we did in the earlier demonstration exercises, as if trying to detect minute changes in air movement and temperature. This stimulates the energy structures contained in the hands. The intention to cause erotic stimulation is important to making this work. This changes the quality of the energy projecting from the hands, charging them with sexual energy. The intention and openness to receive erotic energy stimulation is also an important ingredient for successful body awareness lovemaking enhancement.

Feedback from couples experimenting with erotic body awareness energy work shows that both persons must be in tune with the sexual intention for best results. If one person is not open to the idea of having sex at the time and erotic energy stimulation actions are applied, sometimes unpleasant or "creepy" sensations can result. However, sexual interest can also be kindled by such attention. Some experimentation will be necessary to discover what is appropriate for any given situation.

Massage is an excellent way to practice the projection and reception of sexual energy to discover what works best. Acquire some nice massage oil and take turns. The masseur focuses on projecting erotic energy from his hands. The recipient follows the masseur's hands with her body awareness senses, and provides real-time feedback on the energy effects being experienced. The recipient can also experiment with using body awareness to stimulate and energize other erogenous zones during the massage.

With a little experimentation and imagination, various joint energy circuits, like the whole body circuit but involving two people, can also be explored. Body awareness energy work methods can also be used to enhance traditional Tantric sexual practices.

Base Structure—Sacrum/Coccyx

The sacrum area, particularly the coccyx (tailbone), is a sensitive part of the base structure. This area can be stimulated with care during primary center work. Throbbing, buzzing, tingling, and sensations of heat are common. In some people, this area is hypersensitive, especially if Kundalini energy is active. In that case, uncomfortable feelings of pressure and heat can occur, along with electric-feeling spikes of energy shooting up the spine. If strong or painful sensations occur, reduce or avoid stimulation work on this area. (Kundalini-related issues are discussed later.)

Base Structure—Hip Joints

Masses of powerful energy conduits from the legs pass through the thighs and hip joints into the base structure. A large amount of energy flows through the legs, so these structures are robust. When stimulated, the hip joint centers will produce bone-deep throbbing, tingling, and buzzing sensations.

Navel Primary Center

The middle of the navel center is in the belly button. This primary center is larger than the others, usually about the size of a dinner plate, depending on the size of the person. Stimulation actions are therefore larger. When active, this area produces a warm throbbing, tingling, and buzzing sensation in the stomach area. A fluttering, bubbling, windlike feeling of movement inside the stomach can also be produced. When active, this center can stimulate digestive processes.

Solar Plexus Primary Center

The middle of the solar plexus center is in the diaphragm, just below the rib cage and in the sternum. When this center is active, localized throbbing, fluttering, buzzing, and tingling will occur. Stimulation can also cause feelings of pressure and shortness of breath. Breathe slowly and deeply from your belly and this will pass. Reduce the amount of time spent stimulating this area if the feelings become a problem.

Heart Primary Center Structure

The heart primary center is part of a large energy structure in the upper chest. The heart center itself is found in the middle of the chest, in the physical heart. The largest energy vortex flowers in the chest over the front of the heart, with a smaller one to the rear. A pair of robust energy conduits extend out either side under the collarbones and into the shoulders and arms. The arms and hands have a strong

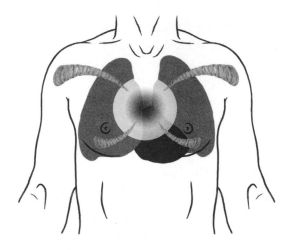

effect on heart center activity. The hand and arm stimulation exercises given earlier will, for example, often cause noticeable increases in heart center activity. When active, the heart center typically produces a light fluttering to throbbing and tingling in the chest over the heart.

Throat Primary Center

The throat primary center sits at the base of the throat where it joins your chest, just above the bony V indent there. When active, this center will throb, tingle, and flutter gently. Because of the sensitive area, body awareness actions and throat center activity can sometimes cause mild choking sensations. Reduce time spent on this area if this feeling becomes a problem, just until the throat center develops and sensations reduce.

Brow Primary Center

The brow primary center sits in the middle of the forehead with its central point between the eyebrow ridges. When active, the frontal energy vortex can expand to the size of a tennis ball, extending into the forehead and the bridge of the nose and into the eyes. This position indicates its relationship with the eyes and the nasal passages.

The brow center is involved with extracting subtle energy from the air we breathe. It is also involved with all levels of mind's eye vision, and is often called the third eye because of this. Related energy centers to this structure also exist in the temples and face. The brow center is strongly connected with the crown center. When active, this center can produce tingling, fluttering, or throbbing sensations in the brow.

Crown Primary Center Structure

The central point of the crown primary center is in the middle of the top of the head. However, the full crown center occupies the whole top of the head above the hairline. The size of the crown center is obvious when fully activated. Stimulation exercises are therefore larger here. The crown center can be likened to the central brain of the energy body. This bears the same relationship with the energy body as does the physical brain with its central nervous system and body. When stimulated to normal levels of activity, this center produces tingling and/or pulsing sensations in the middle of the top of the head.

Stimulating Primary Centers

The best way to learn primary center energy work is to do it yourself. Following are the basic stimulation methods, most of them described earlier. After this, a variety of other stimulation methods are introduced, some for stimulating individual primary centers and some for stimulating the whole energy body.

Preparing for a Primary Center Session

To prepare for primary center energy work, first choose a time and place where you will not be disturbed for the duration of your session. Put aside at least 30 minutes. Sit comfortably in loose clothing, kick off your shoes, and place your feet on a cushion. Carry out the physical relaxation exercise given earlier, tensing and relaxing muscle groups, and then pre-stimulate your hands, arms, feet, and legs, and do a whole body bounce. Finish by doing awareness belly breathing for a few minutes until your mind is quiet and relaxed.

Continue each stimulation action for 30 seconds to one minute or until you feel noticeable sensations in the energy center you are working upon, and then move on to the next center. Spend more time using actions that produce greater stimulation. Spend more time on energy centers that produce few or no sensations. Experiment with the speed and intensity of energy ball actions to find what works best. The goal is to stimulate each energy center to a light level of activity. Once throbbing and/or tingling is felt, consider that center to be active and move on. The colors of the energy balls used below correspond with the color of the energy produced by each center.

Raising Energy to Primary Centers

When you are ready to begin, start by forming energy balls in your feet. Use these to sweep energy up your legs several times to your base center, the perineum. Imagine and feel as if you are sweeping, sponging, and pulling water up your legs and pushing it into your base primary center. Flick your awareness back to your feet and repeat the upward energy sweep.

Repeat the energy sweep process several times for each primary center before you use stimulation actions. For example, if you are about to work on your solar plexus center, make several energy sweeps up your legs. Continue this action through your base and navel, and then push the energy into your solar plexus center. Repeat the energy raising process any time you feel it will help.

Base Center Stimulation

Sweep energy several times up your legs to your base center. Focus body awareness in your perineum. Create a red, tennis ball–sized energy ball there and repeatedly move this in and out of the perineum, a few inches inside the body and then a few inches outside, in and out. Next, use the stirring action on the same area, first clockwise and then counterclockwise, and then use the tearing action. Then use a red, expanding and contracting energy ball in your perineum. Finish by breathing a red energy cloud in and out of your base center for several breaths.

Navel Center Stimulation

Sweep energy several times up your legs, through your base, and to your navel center. Focus body awareness in your navel center, in your stomach area. This center is about the size of a dinner plate, so actions are larger. Create a large, orange energy ball and move this back and forth through your stomach. Take it several inches or more outside your body, front and rear. Feel this passing through your body. Next, use the stirring action, clockwise and counterclockwise, and then the tearing action on your navel. Then use a wide wrapping action around your stomach, as if winding a scarf around your waist. Then use a large, orange, expanding and contracting energy ball in your navel. Finish by breathing an orange energy cloud in and out of your navel center for several breaths.

Solar Plexus Center Stimulation

Sweep energy several times up your legs, through your base and navel, and to your solar plexus center. Focus body awareness in your solar plexus center. Create a yellow, tennis ball–sized energy ball and move this back and forth through your body, taking it several inches outside front and back. Feel this passing through your body. Next, use a stirring action, clockwise and counterclockwise, and then a tearing action. Then use a wrapping action around your lower chest. Then use a yellow, expanding and contracting energy ball in your solar plexus. Finish by breathing a yellow energy cloud in and out of your solar plexus center for several breaths.

Heart Center Stimulation

Sweep energy several times up your legs, through your base, navel, and solar plexus, and to your heart center. Focus body awareness in your heart center. Create a green, tennis ball–sized energy ball and move this back and forth through your heart and chest, taking it several inches or more outside, front and back. Feel this passing through your body. Next, use a stirring action, clockwise and counterclockwise, and then a tearing action. Then use a wrapping action around your upper chest. Then use a green, expanding and contracting energy ball in your heart. Finish by breathing a green energy cloud in and out of your heart center for several breaths.

Throat Center Stimulation

Sweep energy several times up your legs, through your base, navel, solar plexus, and heart, and to your throat center. Focus body awareness in your throat center. Create a blue, tennis ball–sized energy ball and move this back and forth through your throat, taking it several inches or more outside, front and back. Feel this passing through your body. Next, use a stirring action, clockwise and counterclockwise, and then a tearing action. Then use a wrapping action, as if winding a scarf around your neck. Then use a blue, expanding and contracting energy ball in your throat. Finish by breathing a blue energy cloud in and out of your throat center for several breaths.

Brow Center Stimulation

Sweep energy several times up your legs, through your base, navel, solar plexus, heart, and throat, and to your brow center. Focus body awareness in your brow center. Create a purple, golf ball–sized energy ball and move this back and forth through your head at the brow level. Feel this moving through your brain and several inches outside the front and back of your head. Next, create another purple energy ball and move this from temple to temple, feeling it moving through your brain. Bounce the ball back and forth through your brain, feeling it moving several inches outside each side. Next, use a wide brushing action from side to side across your whole forehead, and then brush it up and down over your brow from just above your hairline to the tip of your nose. Then use a stirring action, clockwise and counterclockwise, and then a tearing action. Next, use a wrapping action as if winding a bandage around your head. Then use a purple, expanding and contracting energy ball in your brow. Finish by breathing a purple energy cloud in and out of your brow center for several breaths.

Crown Center Stimulation

Sweep energy several times up your legs, through your base, navel, solar plexus, heart, throat, and brow, and to your crown center. Focus body awareness on your crown center. The crown center occupies the whole top of your head above the hairline, but it flowers at a point in the middle of your head. Create a violet, tennis ball–sized energy ball there. Move it down through your brain to your neck, and then to several inches above your head. Feel this moving inside your head. Next, use a large stirring action as if painting the whole top of your head above the hairline with a four-inch paintbrush, clockwise and then counterclockwise. Then use a large tearing action, as if you were pulling your scalp in two with your hands, repeatedly. Next, use a large, violet, expanding and contracting energy ball in the top part of your head. Then feel and imagine that you are repeatedly bouncing a large, heavy, violet energy ball off the top of your head, like a soccer ball. Finish by breathing a violet energy cloud into and out of your crown center for several breaths.

Closing Primary Centers

Primary energy centers do not need to be closed after they have been stimulated. They are not little mechanical doors that can be opened and closed. Nor can they be closed or deactivated by reversing the actions that were used to activate them. Further stimulation will always result. The best ways to reduce primary center activity, if noticeable activity continues after a session, are breaking relaxation discipline, physical activity, and eating. Get up, raid the refrigerator, go for a walk, take a cool shower, or take a nap. Everything will go back to normal. Deactivating primary energy centers and grounding practices are dealt with later in this book.

Extra Primary Center Stimulation Actions

Some of the following techniques are for stimulating individual primary energy centers; others are for stimulating the entire energy body. These methods can be added to your primary center energy work sessions as they are learned and as necessary to provide extra stimulation. Experiment with the speed and intensity of these actions. Remember to stay in touch with your body at all times and feel these body awareness actions moving on or through your body.

Hip Bounce

Create an energy ball the size of a tennis ball over your left hip joint. Imagine this to be heavy and full of water. Move the energy ball through your body and out of the right hip joint. Take this several inches or more outside your body on either side. Bounce this ball side to side through your hips. Experiment with the speed and intensity of this action. Bounce it slow and intense, and then hard and fast. Continue for two minutes or longer, or until energy sensations are felt.

Groin Bounce

Create a heavy, tennis ball–sized energy ball just above your pubic area. Bounce this through your body at a slight downward angle to your tailbone, and then back to the start. Repeat this, bouncing the energy ball back and forth through your body, repeatedly. Vary the speed and intensity of the bounce action. Continue for one minute, or until energy sensations are felt. Discontinue this action if it causes erotic sensations.

Head Circuits

Apart from the crown and brow centers, the head and face and neck contain many important energy structures, including the ears, eyes, nasal, and mouth areas. The following methods stimulate the entire head, inside and out. Make up some new actions of your own.

Head Spins

This action stimulates all of the energy centers in your head and face, including the brow and crown centers. Create an elongated energy ball, like a large banana, positioned vertically beside your head, from the top of your head to your chin. Imagine that this is connected by many flexible energy filaments to the middle line inside

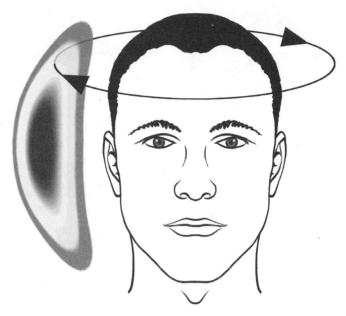

your head. Move this energy shape clockwise around your head. Keep this action close to your skin, feeling it moving the full length of your head and face as you move it around and around. Continue for one minute or longer.

Speed up the action and feel this energy shape moving three feet away from your head, as it would in real life with centrifugal force. Speed it up more and feel it spinning around your head several feet out. Imagine and feel this whooshing as it spins around your head. Experiment with the speed. Try the reverse direction, slow and fast.

Head Rolls

Create a horizontal, elongated energy shape like a banana in front of your face. Hold this close to your face, feeling it all the way as it moves. Move it down over your face, over and under your chin, through your neck, up and over the back of your head to the top, and back to the start, moving it around and around. Stay in touch with this action as the energy shape moves. Experiment with the speed. Continue for one minute or more. Reverse the direction and repeat.

Create a banana energy shape on the left side of your head, over your ear. Keep this action close to your head. Move this up and over

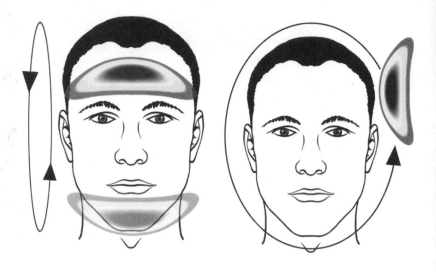

your head, down the right side, and through your neck, around and around. Experiment with the speed. Continue for one minute or more. Reverse the direction and repeat.

Head Wrap

Create an energy roll, like a big roll of four-inch bandage, and feel this close to your head. Feel and imagine this unwinding as it moves over your head, around and around. Move this as if you were bandaging your entire head, from neck to crown like an Egyptian mummy. Continue this for one minute or more.

Head Bounce

Create a golf ball–sized energy ball over your brow center, as we did earlier. Bounce this through and out of the back of your head, feeling it moving through the substance of your brain. Bounce the ball back and forth, progressively extending the distance outside your body until you are touching the walls before you and behind you at the end of each bounce. If lying down, bounce from ceiling and floor. Try to stay in touch with where the ball is in your room as it moves. Just a basic impression of where it is at each moment will suffice. Vary the speed of the bounce action. Continue for one minute or longer.

Repeat this exercise on your temples, with a side to side wall bounce.

Tongue Massage

Open your mouth and poke out your tongue, and then let it relax. Hold your mouth slightly open with your tongue resting slightly out. Create an energy ball over the tip of your tongue and move it into your mouth over your tongue to the back of your throat. Bounce the energy ball through your tongue from tip to base, back and forth. Vary the bounce speed. Continue for one minute or more. This action will cause a slightly salty and metallic taste, similar to that caused by touching both poles of a small battery to your tongue.

Whole Body Stimulation Actions

The following actions are more advanced. The plank and two tubes methods provide whole body stimulation. The spinal and central channel bounce methods provide strong stimulation of the roots of all primary energy centers. Other uses for the plank will be given later in this book.

The Plank

The plank technique is extremely versatile. It can be used to stimulate your whole energy body, to clear your personal space and the atmosphere around you, and even to create energy shields. This technique is best learned with your body straight, either standing up or lying down. If standing, have one hand on a chair or wall and take care, as this exercise can cause dizziness.

Stage 1

Close your eyes and create a thick energy strip beside you that runs the whole length of your body. Imagine and feel that you have a heavy plank or post of wood standing beside you, touching your whole body down one side. Imagine and feel that this plank is attached to your central channel by hundreds of flexible energy filaments, like invisible rubber bands.

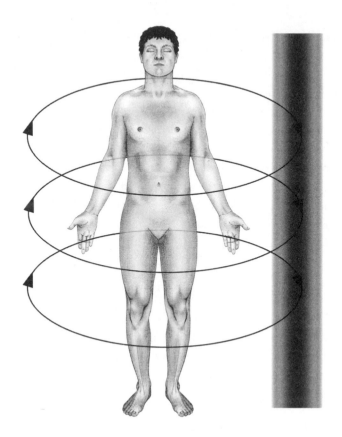

Move the plank clockwise around your body, staying in touch with it and feeling it the full length of your body. Increase the speed of the plank action, and as it speeds up, imagine and feel that centrifugal force is causing the plank to move further out from your body. The faster you move the plank, the further out from your body it flies. The invisible rubber bands stretch infinitely. Imagine the plank whooshing through the air around your body, as it would if the plank were real. Vary the speed of the plank action. Feel it come in close to your body when it is slow, and feel it move out when it is faster. Continue for two minutes or longer.

Stage 2

Spend some time playing with your plank, slow and fast. When you get used to this, speed up and move your plank out further until it is filling your room and almost touching the walls around you. Maintain a basic awareness of where the plank is as it moves around your body, imagining and feeling where it is as it moves past walls, windows, doors, et cetera. Continue for two minutes or longer.

Spin the plank even faster and take it beyond your walls, out into your garden, out over your town, out over the horizon, out into deep space, sweeping the edges of the universe. Continue for two minutes or longer.

Spin your plank clockwise around you, moving it in and out for a minute. Then stop it cold and spin it counterclockwise. This is difficult as the plank action very quickly gains body awareness momentum, but reversing the action has excellent willpower training value.

Once the plank technique is learned, it can be done with eyes open or closed, in any position (while sitting, standing, walking, et cetera).

Caution: Take it easy with the spinal and central channel bounce and two tube actions, which are coming up next. Stop if energy sensations become too strong, particularly if you feel strong cramping, burning, or pressure sensations in your groin or tailbone. Reduce time and intensity spent with these actions if the sensations become a problem.

Spinal Bounce

This method stimulates the spinal channel and the roots of all primary energy centers. Pre-stimulate, and then focus body awareness in the tip of your tailbone. Feel and imagine an electric blue, tennis ball–sized energy ball forming there. Imagine and feel this ball move up your spine to the top of your head, and then back down to your coccyx. Use a bounce speed of about one-half to one second up and the same down. Vary the speed to find what is most effective. Continue bouncing for two minutes or longer. Increase the bounce to as fast and as powerful as you can for the final ten seconds, and then stop.

Extended Spinal Bounce

Perform a comfortable spinal bounce, as above, and then extend this down into the earth below you and up into the sky above you.

Push the bounce action further and further up and down. Imagine and feel that you are bouncing to the center of the Earth, and up into outer space. Continue for two minutes or longer.

Central Channel Bounce

This action helps clear and nurture the development of your central channel. It also stimulates the roots of all primary energy centers. Pre-stimulate, and then form a tennis ball– sized energy ball in your perineum. Move the energy ball up through the center of your torso, through your throat, out of the top of your head, and then back down to your perineum. Bounce at a comfortable speed of about one-half to one second either way. Stay in touch with where your energy ball is, feeling it moving up and down through the inside your body. Continue for two minutes or longer.

Extended Central Channel Bounce

Perform a comfortable central channel bounce, as above. Then extend the bounce action to the center of the Earth and up into outer space. Continue for two minutes or longer.

Two Tubes

Two tubes is a more difficult technique, so please do not expect to master it in one session. It gets easier with practice. This method stimulates your whole energy field, inside and outside your body. My best advice is for you to not think about how you will do this. Let go of your physical limitations and just do this. Most people need several sessions before it becomes workable, so please persevere. This method is best learned standing or lying down with eyes closed. Once learned, it can be done in a sitting position with eyes open.

Stage 1

To begin, imagine and feel you are inside a full length tube of energy, like a glass tube that fits snugly over your body, open at both ends. Imagine and feel this tube spinning clockwise around your body. Feel this with the full length of your whole body as best you can. Do not feel just one part of it moving around you, like with the plank

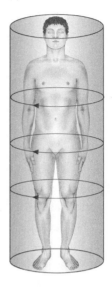
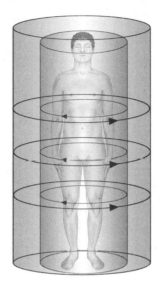

method. Imagine and feel the whole tube spinning with your entire body. Spend some time getting used to this action before attempting Stage 2.

Stage 2

Imagine and feel you are inside a larger tube of energy that is full body length and about one arm's length from your body. Imagine and feel this spinning counterclockwise around you. Imagine and feel this moving with your whole body. Hold this spinning tube as best you can until you get used to the action.

Stage 3

Perform Stage 1 and have the smaller energy tube spinning clockwise around your body. Hold this action until it gains body awareness momentum and stabilizes. Next, create the second larger tube an arm's length from your body and make this spin counterclockwise. Continue spinning both tubes simultaneously, the inner tube clockwise and the outer tube counterclockwise. Continue this for a few minutes or longer.

The two tubes method stimulates the entire energy body, but it has a more pronounced effect on the central channel and on the roots of all primary energy centers. This encourages primary energy centers to activate more fully. The opposing clockwise and counterclockwise directions can be reversed. Try this and sense which direction feels best to you.

Energy Work Issues

This section deals with common issues and problems that can arise through the practice of body awareness development exercises.

While primary centers may become active and produce noticeable throbbing and tingling sensations during practice sessions, there may not be any noticeable spiritual phenomena. This can be likened to starting the engine of an automobile but not engaging the gears. It will just sit there ticking over, waiting for someone to drive it away. Spiritual abilities and phenomena take time to grow, barring natural ability. Energy work encourages this growth process. Your intentions are also important and frequent affirmations—like, "I have visions," "I am clairvoyant," and "I see energy," et cetera—will help.

A consideration for energy work is how much work should be done on each of the primary energy centers. Extra work on higher centers is often necessary to excite them into activity. But it is unwise to focus too much on a higher center. Most potential problems that could arise from overworking higher centers can be avoided by using common sense and exercising the whole energy body in a balanced way.

The base center is the first structure to target for development. Extra stimulation in this area will help the whole energy body. When this center begins to activate, noticeable tingling and/or throbbing and pressure sensations will be felt in the perineum area. Once this is achieved, extra stimulation should be applied to the navel center during practice sessions. When both the base and navel centers are noticeably lightly active, the solar plexus should be the next target for extra stimulation, and then the heart, throat, brow, and crown. In this way, primary centers will develop more evenly and the likelihood of imbalance problems will be minimized.

Most people undertaking energy work will experience only mild sensations to begin with. Light sensation—slight pulsing and tingling sensations—are excellent for general energy work and development, but everyone is different and some people have more sensitive energy bodies than others. The following sections focus on the most common issues that can arise and what can be done to maintain sensible energetic balance.

Energy work can cause a variety of weird sensations. The most common primary center–related sensations include throbbing, pulsing, tingling, and fluttering. Other feelings include localized warm and cool sensations, mild cramping, tightness, heaviness, and pressure. Active primary energy centers and structures affect nerves and surrounding muscles in unusual ways, often causing localized muscular twitching and spasms. Strong throbbing energy center activity can be felt by touching the area with your fingertips, showing that these are physical sensations, and therefore, involve physical nerves and muscles.

Strong sensations, pressures, and pains are usually caused by energy centers and structures awakening from dormancy. This is generally only a temporary condition, like using muscles that have not been worked out for a long time. If uncomfortable or painful symptoms appear, the golden rule should be applied: Stop and take a break from energy work until everything is back to normal, and then return to energy work a little more gently. Strong sensations will always reduce with practice. How long this takes varies greatly, but most sensations will reduce significantly within a few days or so.

If pain persists in any area when you do energy work, avoid direct stimulation there. If pain persists outside energy work sessions, it would be wise to seek the opinion of a medical doctor to check if a physical problem is involved. Sometimes body awareness–based energy work will bring physical ailments out into the open.

Reduced Sensations

When energy work is first undertaken, it is common to experience strong intermittent energy sensations for the first few weeks. These sensations soon reduce. When this happens, many people think they are doing something wrong or that the practice is not working anymore. But this is perfectly normal. Do not judge energy body activity and development by the strength of the sensations you feel. Strong sensations will *always* reduce as the energy body, and the physical body and its nerves, adapt and evolve.

Energy Work Tiredness

We live in a veritable ocean of subtle energies. On average, people absorb only a fraction of what is available to them each day, and this steadily reduces with age. Let us say that you normally absorb 100 units of subtle energy (raw vitality) per day, but when you start doing energy work you begin using 200 units per day. The deficit of 100 units will be made up from your energy body's storage areas, and physical tiredness can result. This happens because your energy body is using more energy than it is absorbing.

This is much like what happens if you live a sedentary life and suddenly begin working out in the gym every day. You would understandably have sore muscles, be more hungry, and need more sleep for several weeks, until your physical body adapts to the new regime.

With a little time and regular energy work, your energy body will adapt, evolve, and overcome the energy deficit by absorbing and storing more energy. As this happens, you will begin to feel more energized and more in tune with life. This is much like how a new physical exercise regime and healthy diet take some time before everything stabilizes and you start to feel better.

Brow and Crown Center Pressure and Pain

Early brow and crown center activity periodically can produce uncomfortable and even painful symptoms while these centers are coming out of dormancy. Not everyone will experience this, and the intensity will vary from person to person. But most people should expect to experience some level of this for a short time. This problem is always temporary and intermittent. While you should not expect this, it is best to be aware of the possibilities and what can be done to help.

Strong primary center pressure sensations are like growing pains. They can be intense at times, but they are no real cause for alarm. For example, a typical early brow center sensation is a point of intense pressure, as if someone were pressing a thumb hard into the middle of your forehead. A tight band of pressure around the whole circumference of your head at brow level is also common, as is pressure over the entire head.

Brow and crown center pressures and pains will not damage you, but they may at times cause painful tension headaches. If this happens, treat these as you would normally treat a headache. Consult a medical doctor if pain persists.

Cobwebs Sensations

Stimulating the energy body, especially the higher centers, can cause supporting energy structures to activate in a noticeable way. The facial area is extremely sensitive and some unusual sensations can result. While these are rarely intense enough to be actually painful, they can be uncomfortable and distracting. This sensation is commonly called cobwebs.

Cobweb-like tickling, tingling, and stinging sensations will often be felt in the facial area. These may start at any time, even during light relaxation and meditation, which causes increased energy flow. This can also happen while you are trying to fall asleep. This can feel like mosquitoes crawling over your face, with some of them biting and stinging. There may be only one or two tickling or stinging areas. The majority of people will get at least some minor cobweb sensations during energy work sessions, particularly when combined with physical and mental relaxation exercises.

It is likely that energy flowing over and through supporting structures in the facial area overstimulates the nerves there, causing the cobweb sensations. The best way to handle cobwebs is to ignore them. Try to resist the urge to scratch, as this will break your concentration and disturb your relaxed state. Scratching also disrupts sensitive subtle energy structures that spread out over the facial area. This tends to reduce brow and crown center activity. Check your room for insects before each session if this is an ongoing problem, as this eliminates that possibility.

A sensation similar to cobwebs can appear directly over the site of any Chakra. This is a tickling, tingling sensation. This signals that a center is active at a more refined level than that which produces throbbing and pulsing sensations.

Reducing Primary Center Activity

As said, it is unnecessary to close or deactivate primary energy centers after stimulating them. Attempts to do this by reversing the method used to stimulate them will always cause further stimulation. Primary centers begin deactivating naturally the moment you break your relaxed state. Sensations will usually cease within a few minutes.

If primary center activity continues after energy work sessions, there will always be good reasons for this. For example, energy blockages may have cleared and so energy continues flowing to heal and restore depleted energy body structures. In this case, primary centers will continue working to produce the necessary energy. This can also happen spontaneously at any time as a byproduct of progressive energy work, the clearing of energy blockages, and spiritual development.

In cases where strong or uncomfortable sensations continue, here are some ways to reduce activity:

• Avoid focusing body awareness on your energy body.
• Eat something substantial.
• Perform physical exercise such as walking, jogging, swimming, et cetera.
• Lie on the ground and feel and imagine energy draining away.
• Take a nap or go to bed for the night.
• Take a cool shower.
• Avoid energy work until sensations cease.

Heavy physical exercise to the point of exhaustion will ground you and drain your energy body of all excess energy. This will deactivate your energy body and stop all energy movement sensations, including heavier types of Kundalini-related activity.

Body Rush Sensations

It is not uncommon to experience occasional tingling, adrenaline-like rushes of energy up through the body, especially through the back area, while doing energy work. Uplifting music and prose can also cause similar sensations and are due to an emotional response. Many things, including energy raising and the spontaneous release of energy blockages, can trigger surges through the energy body. These tingling energy waves can be quite strong, even breathtaking at times, but they are perfectly normal for persons undertaking energy body and spiritual development work.

Astral Projection

Another cause of energy surges is spontaneous astral projections, which often happen unnoticed during meditation and relaxation sessions. Deep relaxation and meditation always involve some level of an altered state of consciousness. The mind awake/body asleep state allows astral projection to occur. (Astral projection is a natural phenomenon that occurs every time you sleep.) It happens unnoticed during the mind awake/body asleep state because of the mind-split effect.

At the start of an astral projection, the mind splits into two distinct parts. The original copy of mind and memory always stays within the physical body while it lives. During astral projection, an energy copy of your mind is generated and projected out of body. In the mind awake/body asleep state, the physical body/mind remains active, even though the physical body is technically asleep. During an astral projection, both aspects of mind, physical and astral, simultaneously exist and function independently from each other. This creates two memory sets for the same time period, which is what causes the astral memory recall problem.

After the astral double returns and reintegrates with its physical body/mind, the strongest copy of memory will always form the recallable memory, the final wrinkle. Through constant use, the physical body/mind has much stronger habitual memory storage and recall pathways than does its astral double. So, usually it is the memories of the physical body/mind that are stored and recalled. The lost astral projection memories are then downloaded into subconscious memory storage, and usually lost to the recall ability of the conscious mind.

For more information on astral projection, please see my book *Astral Dynamics: A NEW Approach to Out-of-Body Experience* (Hampton Roads, 1999).

Rousing Dormant Primary Centers

While you may feel activity in some primary centers right away, others may lie dormant even after intensive regular stimulation. The secondary and tertiary structures of the energy body play a significant part in primary center activity. It is rare not to have any primary center response at all. Often, it is simply a matter of spending more time working on dormant primary centers. Most important to activate and bring online is the base primary center. When this is active, more energy will flow to higher centers, which will cause them to begin developing.

Your physical health and fitness will affect the responsiveness of your energy body. A sedentary lifestyle sometimes causes the accumulation of heavy, *stuck* energy. This can make it more difficult to rouse the energy body into activity. If none of your primary centers respond at all after a few weeks of regular energy work, a healthier diet and better exercise for a few weeks can make all the difference.

Overworking Energy Centers

Your energy body is intimately connected with your physical body and mind. What affects one will affect the other. It is okay to spend extra time working on dormant primary centers. But it is unwise to get into the habit of working only on higher centers. For example, if you regularly spend half an hour stimulating your brow center and only five minutes on the others, this can cause psychic and mental imbalance and headaches. In the same way, focusing too much on the heart center can cause emotional problems, including increased emotional sensitivity, mood swings, anxiety, or depression. These problems are usually only temporary, as long as common sense and the golden rule of energy work are applied.

Kundalini-Related Issues

Note: Some of the ideas offered here concerning Kundalini may differ from traditional practices and schools of thought. This is because my thoughts come largely from personal experience.

Kundalini is the Eastern term for an evolutionary energy mechanism that is built into everyone. This natural evolutionary mechanism is inherent to all of humanity, regardless of race, belief, spiritual tradition or practice. When this mechanism activates, persons are said to have awakened Kundalini or to have Kundalini rising. In the Western world today, the traditional meaning of the word Kundalini has been popularly expanded to describe most subtle energy-related sensations. In this sense, anyone experiencing energy sensations from the work in this book could be said to have active or awakened Kundalini.

However, Kundalini activity in the traditional sense is a natural phenomenon that ultimately goes hand in hand with spiritual and energy body development. While awakening Kundalini is not the specific purpose of this book, energy work can trigger this type of activity in some people. This is nothing to be afraid of, and it is impossible to completely avoid.

Kundalini is an energy seed that exists in the base of the spine, in the sacrum. This is traditionally depicted as a small cobra snake coiled three-and-a-half times in the sacrum. This can be awakened through spiritual practices, energy work, and intellectual activity. When this happens, Kundalini is said to rise. Kundalini is the quintessence of spiritual evolution. Once awakened, this mechanism begins to evolve the consciousness of the person involved—spiritually and energetically—and enhance spiritual and psychic sensitivity.

In the traditional sense, if Kundalini *rises* spontaneously, it will first cause Kundalini *spikes*. These spikes are intense and often painful electrical-like burning sensations that shoot up the spine. Do not confuse these symptoms with normal adrenaline-like energy rushes as associated with normal energy work and emotional responses.

Full spontaneous Kundalini rising is rare and not something to be overly concerned about. It usually takes many years of mental preparation, energy work, and intellectual and spiritual practice to trigger significant levels of Kundalini activity. (Carl Gustav Jung, the famous Swiss psychiatrist and founder of analytical psychology, claimed to have experienced a spontaneous Kundalini rising. He wrote extensively on the primary energy centers, or major Chakras, and Kundalini.)

The word Kundalini is popularly used to describe most subtle energy-related sensations. So, a new term was needed to describe the main event. By this I mean a full Kundalini rising, which I first experienced in 1990. I call this event *Uraeus Serpent of Fire*. Uraeus is the golden headpiece of Egyptian gods, like Amon Ra, which depicts a coiled cobra with its rampant head rising over the brow. I think this depicts fully raised Kundalini, making it an obvious descriptive choice. The snake entwined staff of the caduceus symbol shown earlier also hints at Kundalini rising.

Kundalini can rise in a number of ways. It can involve a single primary center at a time, with each center activating separately, or all

centers together. These events can be minutes, hours, or even years apart. These differences arise from the many variables of a person's energy body makeup, including energy blockages and the level of spiritual development of the person at that time.

When Kundalini Uraeus rises to the full, the event begins with intense electrical burning spikes of energy shooting up through the spine, called Kundalini spikes. Next comes a massive column of energy shooting up through the central channel. After this, the serpent energy sensation rises up through the body. This feels like a physical snake as thick as a man's wrist is forcing its way up through the perineum, coiling three-and-a-half times clockwise up through the torso (around the central channel), and then up through the neck and head. When this reaches the head, an intense, brilliant flash of light occurs in the mind's eye. This is a massive brow center strobe.

The rising serpent is a visceral, internal sensation and the stomach will physically contort at times during the event. This is uncomfortable, but not painful. It is, I think, caused by an internal snakelike manifestation of ectoplasm. (Ectoplasm is a semisolid, etheric substance that can be produced by the energy body.) After this, it feels as if the crown and brow centers temporarily fuse. It then feels like a heavy flap of flesh is hanging down over the eyes and nose. Kundalini is described as a cobra because the sensations involved feel like the movements of a cobra. This event involves physical and energy sensations; so, the cobra is not just symbolic analogy, it is descriptive of the event.

The term *raising Kundalini* is a bit misleading, as it is more descriptive to say that Kundalini is *triggered* or *released*. It can be difficult or impossible to stop the main event once it is triggered. Early sensations can be intense and painful. They remain intense, but they are only painful during the first few major events.

Another point of note is that Kundalini is not a *raise once and it's done* phenomenon that brings instant enlightenment and full psychic abilities. Persons may achieve full enlightenment of consciousness during a successful Kundalini raising session, but this will be abstract and temporary. After the session, they will revert to normal consciousness. This event will, however, change persons in many ways because the process of spiritual evolution will greatly intensify.

The words *enlightenment* and *illumination* accurately describe not only a massive brow center strobe, but also changes inside the mind's eye. This level of spiritual development causes light to appear in the mind's eye. By this I mean that when the eyes are closed, light will be seen as coming from above. However, while enlightenment is only temporarily achieved as abstract God consciousness when

Kundalini rises to the crown center during a session, spiritual and psychic abilities and the intellect will begin to grow. Persons in this situation will begin to develop inner genius. How this genius manifests will depend upon a person's nature. They may, for example, become musical, artistic, literary, or scientific geniuses, depending upon natural inclinations.

Kundalini involves a new level of energy body activity, which includes but goes beyond the primary center level. Raised Kundalini must be developed after it has been achieved. After the initial main event, Kundalini evolves with each subsequent Uraeus serpent of fire experience. Beyond the first few events, more phenomena will occur, including the Medusa and Aummm effects.

The Medusa effect is my term to describe a Kundalini Uraeus phenomenon. This feels like the whole top of the head disappears and hundreds of fat, snakelike antennae extend from the surface of the brain. These feel like they are as intimately connected with one as one's fingers. This is a weird but comfortable sensation. These antennae form specific geometric patterns, which I think relate to what are traditionally called mandalas. These patterns respond to thoughts, and the patterns change as one's thoughts change. Some antennae will point to the object of the thought in the real world, if there is an object. For example, if you think of a real person, a mandala will form and some of the antennae will point to where that person is physically located.

The Aummm effect is my term for another phenomenon. This begins to manifest along with or after the Medusa effect is established. This feels and sounds like a deep, solid, "aummm" sound vibrating all around and through you. This is a constant sound and vibration, like would come from the throats of many mature men in a cave vibrating and resonating the "aummm" sound.

The most common warning related to Kundalini is that it can cause intense and lasting sexual arousal. While this can occur, it is rare and nothing to be overly concerned about. I have only encountered a very small number of problems relating to this, and only two were acute. Most common problems involving energy work and sexual arousal are only mild and temporary. That is, of course, if common sense and the golden rule of energy work are followed.

Primary Center Strobing

Two major functions of all primary energy centers are to *transform* energy and to *accumulate* energy. When a primary center accumulates enough energy, it reaches a critical mass and releases that energy in an energetic burst. This burst is what I call the strobe effect.

All primary energy centers have the ability to strobe. They can strobe independently or in groups. A primary center strobe involves a Kundalini level of energy activity, but this may not involve any other aspect of Kundalini. When the base center strobes, a Kundalini spike will be experienced if energy shoots up the spine and/or central channel. The base, brow, and heart primary centers produce the most noticeable sensations when they strobe independently. When a primary energy center strobes, this indicates that a significant change has occurred. This may involve it awakening out of dormancy or evolving.

The intense burst of energy from a strobing primary center can flash activate heavy-duty energy circuitry that did not exist a moment before. High-level energy activity occurs within and around that primary energy center. This can affect other primary energy centers. This can also cause spontaneous psychic and spiritual abilities and phenomena to manifest. However, often nothing apparent may happen beyond the strobe event itself.

Brow/Crown Center Strobe

An occasional result of primary center development involves the brow and crown centers. This phenomenon involves a flash of brilliant light in the mind's eye, seen with the eyes open or shut. This is like a powerful camera flash going off at close range. This is usually accompanied by a mild feeling of concussion over the whole facial area, as if one has been struck hard with a pillow. This shows the involvement of facial energy structures relating to brow and crown centers. It also demonstrates that a single primary center can strobe independently.

A brow center strobe indicates that the brow center is more highly evolved than average. This is caused by the brow center strobing, much like a capacitor releasing energy. This will not cause any harm, and it is an excellent sign if one is interested in higher spiritual and psychic development. The strobe effect is related to Kundalini in the traditional sense. This is known to occur when Kundalini rises to the brow and crown centers.

Brow center strobes can happen to anyone, even to people who have never done any kind of developmental work. It can happen to some people while they are trying to sleep, or they may awaken to a brow center strobe. This can happen any time, even while in the shower, but is more likely to occur in a relaxed state. Some of the cases I have been presented with have involved teenagers who were in the early stages of learning meditation and energy work.

The strobe effect can be frightening if you do not know what is happening. Having no other explanation or point of reference, many people think they have experienced a malevolent attack by an unseen entity. But this is not the case. This is a natural energy phenomenon and an excellent sign of spiritual development. This also indicates the presence of strong visual mind's eye ability, although this may be unrealized at the time.

Purple Brow Center Strobe

Another version of the brow center strobe involves a brilliant flash of purple light in the mind's eye. This happened to my son Jesse when he was 14 years old. He was in the shower and I was working in my office at the other end of the house. He yelled out to me loudly a few times. I listened and was about to investigate when he ran into my office dripping water everywhere. He excitedly told me, "Dad, Dad. The world's gone purple, man! Everything's purple, man!"

Once I calmed him down, Jesse told me a fascinating tale. He said that while showering, for no apparent reason, he felt a kind of a thud or concussion in his forehead and his vision flooded with brilliant, thick, purple light. This was a shock and he yelled out, but it did not hurt. For several seconds after this he could see nothing but purple light. Then it faded and his vision returned, but everything was tinged and outlined with purple light. Jesse said it was like there was a sticky purple gas clinging to everything. He held up his hands and said he could still see purple around his hands and arms. I was fascinated and looked at Jesse's aura. It was expanded and all I could see was a huge blob of brilliant purple light surrounding him. This was totally different from the last time I had viewed it, several days earlier.

This tale progressed later that day, as the effects of the purple brow center strobe became apparent. Jesse liked to draw and doodle, as most children do, but his drawings were very average. A few hours later that same day, though, Jesse was watching TV and doodling as I worked in my office. Again he yelled out to me "Dad, Dad. Quick! Come and see! Come and see!" I went into the living room and Jesse was excitedly drawing, copying a fairly complex magazine picture. But the copy he was creating was stunning. It was perfect. He could not understand how, but suddenly he just started drawing at a skill level way beyond his normal ability.

In a proverbial nutshell, the long-term result was that Jesse became an artist at the moment of the purple brow center strobe. The purple strobe released his dormant creative and psychic abilities. On that day, he became extremely creative and art became his passion. He now passionately pursues a career in art and animation. Jesse's psychic sensitivity and mind's eye abilities also increased that day, and they continue to develop. Some of the illustrations in this book were created by Jesse.

Heart Center Strobe

The heart center can produce strong, visceral sensations under some circumstances. A racing heart sensation can be caused by an astral projection exit. Astral projection often happens unnoticed during relaxation and meditation work, as discussed earlier. This level of heart center activity can be worrisome. But it does not involve the actual physical heart and will not cause any harm.

The heart center can strobe during the act of giving healing. This can also happen during a powerful emotional experience, like falling in love at first sight.

A full heart center strobe during the healing act involves a massive tingling energy surging up through the torso and pulsing down through the arms and into the patient. This event lasts several seconds and the energy has a definite pulsating feel to it as it pumps through the arms and into the patient. The heart center healing method, given later in this book, is based on this phenomenon.

Practice

Do the physical relaxation exercise, tensing and relaxing muscle groups, and then settle yourself with awareness belly breathing. Pre-stimulate your hands and arms and feet and legs. Perform the full body circuit, and then the spinal bounce, central channel bounce, and full body bounce for a minute or so each. Perform the extra hip and base center stimulation actions. Then stimulate each of your primary energy centers, following the instructions given earlier. Finish by doing the plank and two tubes actions for a few minutes each.

The energy work you have done to this point is a voyage of discovery in every sense. I am sure you have already had many interesting energy-related experiences. In the next chapter, we delve into the magical world of consciousness, intention, and energy tools.

FIVE

Charging Energy with Intention

Now that we have explored body awareness and practiced energy work, a new horizon appears. This involves charging body awareness actions with intention and creating and using energy tools. Imagination and intention change the quality and effect of energetic actions.

Consciousness has no boundaries. Imagination, intention, emotion, and energetic actions are all expressions of consciousness. "Where your attention goes your energy flows" is a fundamental principle of energy work. And your energetic actions will always have the properties you imagine and intend them to have.

The nature and use of thought forms, elements, and colors are complex topics in their own rights. The intention here, though, is to introduce a workable understanding of these things to help enhance energy work processes.

All aspects of yourself are interconnected. This is most noticeable at the levels of thought and emotion, as these can profoundly affect your physical body. They also affect your perceptions of life as well as how you interact with your environment and other living beings.

The Water of Life

The pioneering work done by respected researchers like Candace B. Pert and Masaru Emoto on the sensitivity of living molecules to thoughts and emotions makes fascinating reading. Pert shows how thought and emotion affect the human body at the molecular and cellular levels, and how our internal chemistry forms a dynamically interactive information network that links body, mind, and emotion. Emoto shows how water molecules are transformed by thought and intention, and by music and the written word.

> The human body is essentially water, and consciousness is the soul. Methods that help water to flow smoothly are superior to all other medical methods available to us. It's all about keeping the soul in an unpolluted state. Can you imagine what it would be like to have water capable of forming beautiful crystals flowing throughout your entire body? It can happen if you let it.
>
> Among all medicines, there are none with the healing powers of love. Since I came to this realization, I have continued to tell people that *immunity* is love. What could be more effective at overcoming negative powers and returning vitality to the body? (Emoto and Thayne 2005)

Emoto's work is famous for showing how molecules of water are transformed when they are exposed to intention. Some of his experiments involve containers of water that have different intentions expressed towards them. Some had been loved and blessed in various ways or had words like "gratitude" and "love" written on them. The water molecules of these samples transformed into beautiful, harmonious, crystalline shapes when frozen, sliced, and observed under a microscope. Water that had been hated or disrespected in some way formed ugly, chaotic shapes. The control group showed no change.

The point here is that as your body is composed mainly of water, Emoto's work can be applied to your body. If you truly express love and gratitude to yourself, the molecules of water of which you are composed will respond by taking on beautiful, harmonious shapes and energy potentials. How you feel about yourself has a direct effect upon your body at the molecular and bioenergetic levels. This suggests that the source of many diseases and illnesses is unhappiness and dissatisfaction with who you are, with disliking yourself. Emoto's work shows that truly loving yourself is a powerful medicine that promotes immunity from disease and good health at the molecular level.

Emoto's research also applies to the human energy body, which is the underlying template of the physical body. Your emotions, thoughts, and intentions directly affect the composition of your energy body, which in turn affects your physical body. This also applies to the composition of anything you create with your thoughts, including body awareness actions, energy constructs, and thought form tools. Energy constructs include all of the energy balls and energy shapes you have already been using. These are, for all intents and purposes, thought forms.

Energy Constructs and Thought Forms

Thought forms are created by the mind and the imagination and are programmed with intention. It is important to recognize the nature of these constructs for what they are so you can make them work better.

An example of creating and programming a thought form is how you created energy balls to sweep and raise energy up to your primary centers. You created these energy balls with your mind and imagination. You programmed these to sweep energy up your legs by *intending* the energy balls to have this effect. Then you applied this by imagining and feeling the energy moving with body awareness actions.

The more attention you pour into an energy construct (thought form) and the more you use it, the more effective it will become.

Affirmations, statements of purpose, and commands are used to empower energy constructs with intention.

Transforming Energy

Body awareness actions and energy constructs can be endowed with different properties and shaped for different purposes with imagination and intention. For example, imagining that an energy ball is a particular color will subtly change the effect it has. Elemental properties (fire, earth, air, water) can also be added. For example, the fire element can be added to an energy ball with the intention of empowering a person or burning away diseased tissue. The water element can be added with the intention of cooling a hot temper or reducing inflammation. The earth element can be added with the intention of grounding a person, countering anxiety, or strengthening bones. The air element can be added with the intention of countering depression or helping with breathing disorders. Mixing and matching colors and elements with intentions will produce different results.

The use of colors and elements is best considered as an optional extra. These are not essential ingredients, but rather additions to the practice of energy work.

Charging with Colors

Using imagination to add color to energy work actions is simple to do. The best way to know the effect of colors is to use them. To begin, experiment with a spectrum of colored energy balls. In the exercises below, observe how the different colors feel. You may feel slightly different textures, warming or cooling, or other energy-related sensations.

Step 1: Create a bright red energy ball between your hands, like we did in the earlier exercise. Move your hands apart and begin bouncing the ball at a comfortable speed from palm to palm. Imagine and feel the vivid, red color of the energy ball. Bounce for a minute or so and observe how it feels. Repeat this with the colors orange, yellow, green, blue, purple, violet, and white. You may notice that each color feels slightly different.

Step 2: Create a vivid, red energy ball over each foot. Bounce at a comfortable speed, one or two seconds either way from feet to hips. Continue for a minute or so. Repeat this exercise with the colors orange, yellow, green, blue, purple, violet, and white. Observe how each color feels.

Experiment with different colors on other areas of your energy body. The degree of sensitivity to colors and elements and the ability to feel magnetic and electric properties varies from person to person. If you cannot feel any difference at this stage, use blue or white for standard energy work unless otherwise specified.

Colors have a considerable effect upon our emotions and energies. Hospitals use pastel colors to calm patients. Fast food joints use brash colors to encourage people to eat and run. Color and lighting are used in advertising to encourage people to buy. Similarly, imagining colored energies can help to refine and/or amplify energy actions and intentions.

Using Color

A basic guide to using color for energy work and healing is given by the colors of the energies generated by the primary energy centers. These are:

- Base: Red
- Navel: Orange
- Solar Plexus: Yellow
- Heart: Green
- Throat: Blue
- Brow: Indigo to Purple
- Crown: Violet

Divide the body into horizontal segments ruled by these colors and use the related primary center color for each area.

Some general examples: Soft pastel colors are best for healing and balancing. Pink is a mixture of colors that carries loving, nurturing energy and can be used on any part of the body. Pastel pink and green help calm the heart center. Imagining a person wrapped in a thick, soft, pink blanket of energy around their shoulders and chest helps convey a warm, soft, cuddly energy. Soft violet and blue help calm the mind. Soft yellow applied to the solar plexus helps calm emotional upsets. The calming effects of these colors can be amplified by combining them with the water element. Imagine pouring a beautiful, translucent liquid of these pastel colors over and into the area you wish to calm.

If a person is low on vital energy, imagine vivid orange and red mixed with the fire element applied to the base and navel primary centers. For grounding as well as reenergizing, imagine molten lava with yellow, orange, and red hues. Lava is a balanced mixture of the earth, fire, and water elements.

When in doubt, use brilliant white. This is a versatile cleansing and balancing color tool, especially if mixed with water or lava. Brilliant white can also be used to clear away toxic energies and remove stubborn energy blocks. To clear toxic energy, imagine the body filling with brilliant white liquid. To clear a blockage, imagine brilliant white lava seeping into the blockage and heating it, causing small explosions within. Feel this happening. The explosions expose new surface areas so that more cleansing lava can penetrate, progressively wearing away toxic energy.

Charging with Elements

Elemental properties can be added to energetic actions and thought form constructs with imagination and intention. The simple use of elements is easy to do, even for a beginner. The addition of elemental analogy enhances the effectiveness of energy work and healing intention. Your astrological birth sign will show you the element to which you are most closely related. Most people find that they can use their birth element more strongly than other elements.

The Elements

The first element is spirit, also called Ether or Akasa. This is the causal spiritual quintessence from which all creative elements spring. The four main creative elements—fire, earth, air, and water—are analogous to the primordial forces that create and sustain the universe. These flow from the causal level into the physical dimension. They combine here in various ways to create all of the different types of matter and energy that exist. All matter and life are mixtures of these energies that are continually moving from spirit into form, through form, and then out of form and back into spirit. This is the great cosmic circle of existence.

The analogous descriptions of the four elements are the closest things we have in the physical universe to describe the creative forces involved. Nothing, no matter or thing, is composed solely of one element. Actual physical fire, air, water, and earth each contain mixtures of all of the elements working together, although obviously the mix varies.

To use these elements, you must learn how to tune into and absorb their energies. This involves tuning into the frequency of each creative energy using analogy, imagination, and your energy senses. It takes a little practice to learn how to tune into these energies to the point where they can be felt and used. The following descriptions will help give you a better feel for this.

Fire Element

Properties: Heating, expanding, consuming, drying, energizing, transforming, and brightening

To absorb the fire element, use the above descriptive words and your own sense experiences with what fire is like. Say the words in your mind and imagine fire from your experience. Imagine this energy as red and fiery. Imagine and feel the essence of fire—the feel, smell, taste, and sound of it—all around you. Feel its heating, expanding, and transforming nature. Absorb all of this from the world around you. Then imagine that the universe around you is composed solely of fire. Take several slow, deep breaths and breathe the fire element into yourself. Feel it soaking into your skin and being absorbed into and filling your body. Then add this element to the energy you are using.

Your body will feel warm as you absorb the fire element. If you feel too warm and are not going to use the fire element, imagine and feel yourself breathing away the fire element until it is all gone.

When I use the fire element, I call on memories of the sun and of bonfires, campfires, and brushfires that I have experienced. I reach out and connect with the fire element and express love and gratitude in return. I draw all this together inside of me with feelings of heat and expansion, and feel this being absorbed into me. I feel myself enveloped in a universe of fire. I breathe this in and feel it soaking into the pores of my skin and filling my body. I then project the energy like a blowtorch flame. For small work, I imagine this energy as a fine-cutting torch; for large work, I imagine a flamethrower.

Water Element

Properties: Cooling, shrinking, moistening, cleansing, diluting, and soothing

To absorb the water element use the above description plus your own sense experiences of what water is like. Say the words in your mind and imagine feelings of water from your own experience. Feel it as being cool, wet, flowing, cleansing, and soothing. Imagine this energy as having a cool, blue-green water color. From your memory, imagine the feeling of rain—of splashing, paddling, swimming, drinking, water gushing from hoses, ocean waves surging and frothing, and the soothing feel of water flowing over your skin. Imagine and feel that you are deep inside an infinite ocean, that the universe around you is only water. Take several long, slow breaths and breathe in the water element. Feel it soaking into your skin and filling your body. Then add this element to the energy you are using.

Your body will feel cool and fluid as you absorb the water element. If you are not going to use the water element, or if you feel too watery, "breathe" the water element away until it is all gone.

When I use the water element, I call on memories of diving in the ocean, walking in the rain, and splashing and sloshing through puddles. I imagine huge ocean waves rising and crashing and bubbling over me. I feel the cool, wet water energy flowing over and being absorbed into me. I imagine the universe around me as pure water. I connect with the water element and express love and gratitude. I pull all of this together inside of me and feel myself absorbing the water element. I then project the energy like water gushing from a hose.

Air Element

Properties: Lightening, floating, windy, blowing, soaring, uplifting, enlivening, and playful

To absorb the air element, use the above description plus your own sense experiences with what air feels like. Say these words in your mind. Imagine and feel air from your own experiences. Imagine this energy as having light, airy, blue color. Imagine and feel the essence of air, the feelings and smells and tastes and sounds of air. Feel its blowing, gusting, uplifting, enlivening, and playful nature. Absorb all of this from the world around you and from the sky. Imagine that the universe around you is pure air like infinite sky. Compress all of these feelings and thoughts into yourself as you absorb the air element. Take several long, slow breaths and breathe in the air element. Feel it soaking into your skin and filling your body. Feel yourself growing lighter and lighter. Then add the air element to the energy you are using.

Your body will feel light and airy as you absorb the air element. If you are not going to use the air element, or if you feel lightheaded, take several breaths and blow it away, imagining and feeling the air element leaving your body until it is all gone.

When I use the air element, I think of children playing with balloons and kites, squealing and running and bouncing with joy. I imagine thousands of airy sparks of energy whizzing around me and bouncing off walls with feelings of playful gusty wind sounds. I call on memories of sheets flapping on washing lines, being buffeted in gales, and the storms from my navy days. I connect with this energy and express love and gratitude. I imagine the universe around me as an infinite sky of moving air. I breathe this in, pull it together inside of me, and absorb the air element. I then project the air element as if from a compressed air hose.

Earth Element

Properties: Heavy, earthy, thickening, grounding, slowing, solidifying, and strengthening

To absorb the earth element, use the above description. Say the words in your mind. Imagine and feel earth from your own sense experiences.

Imagine and feel it as being very heavy, solid, thick, slow, and grounded. Imagine this energy as having earthy brown, gray, and dark colors. Imagine the solid feel of rock and clay and soil with the heavy sensation of gravity. Imagine yourself sinking deep into the planet beneath you until you are surrounded by a universe of earth. Take several long, slow breaths and breathe in the earth element. Feel it soaking into your skin and filling your body from the feet up. Feel yourself growing heavier and heavier as if you are being filled with lead. Compress all of these feelings and thoughts into yourself as you absorb the earth element. Then add this to the energy you are using.

Your body will start feeling heavy as you absorb the earth element. If you are not going to use the earth element and feel too heavy, take several breaths and breathe away the earth element until it is all gone.

When I use the earth element, I call on memories of wheelbarrows full of earth and rocks; the weight, smell, taste, and feel of mud and dirt; and the earthy heaviness of these remembered feelings. I imagine myself sinking into the ground, down into the molten heaviness of the planet core. I feel myself connecting with the energy of the planet that is then all around me. I express love and gratitude towards this. I then breathe in the earth element and feel it soaking into my skin and filling my body. I feel myself growing heavier and heavier as this fills me. It feels like liquid rock or lead is flowing into me as I absorb the earth element. I pull all of this together inside me and add the earth element to the energy I am using. I imagine and feel that I am projecting heavy, crushed rock from a thick, metal pipe.

Elemental energies should not be excessively absorbed. Too much of a single element can disturb one's natural balance. The amount absorbed should be increased progressively, and the excess should be dumped after each practice. Start with ten breaths absorbing an element, and then increase this by two breaths per subsequent practice. Spend a similar time dumping excess elemental energy after each session.

Using Elemental Energy

Elemental energies can be used to strengthen, to heal and balance yourself and other people. Elemental balance is important in a similar way, as it is important to have a balanced diet for good general health. Elemental energies can also be projected into other people. This is a type of healing.

Elements can be compacted into energy balls and then placed inside of yourself or others. This is easy to do, once you can absorb some elemental energy. Mixtures of elements can also be used. The simplest way is to first absorb an element, and then to create an energy ball between your hands, as we did earlier. Cup your hands and imagine and feel the elemental energy pouring into and being compacted into the energy ball. Feel this happening; for example, feel the ball growing heavy for the earth element, warm for the fire, light for the air, and wet for the water. Choose a color for the energy ball that relates to the element being used. When it is finished, feel and imagine yourself placing the ball where it is needed, inside yourself or another person.

Elements can be mixed for different purposes. For example, molten lava is a mixture of fire, water, and earth (earth gains water element when it becomes liquid). Water and air can be mixed by imagining foam or froth. Water, fire, and air can be mixed by imagining hot steam. Water and earth can be mixed by imagining mud or concrete.

Having too much or too little of any element can affect one's personality. Too little air element can cause one to feel depressed, lethargic, and disinterested in life. Too much can cause one to become ungrounded, airheaded, fickle, inconsistent, and silly. Too much earth element can cause heaviness, lethargy, and stuck feelings, slowing the mind and making it difficult to think. Too little can cause one to feel vulnerable, scattered, anxious, lightheaded, and unable to handle life. Too much fire element can cause excessive drive, overconfidence, aggression, and a hot temper. Too little can cause lack of drive and confidence and feelings of insecurity and vulnerability. Too much water element can cause one to vacillate and feel ungrounded, indecisive, and changeable. Too little can cause one to become inflexible, stuck, and hot tempered.

Charging Food, Drink, and Air with Energy and Intention

Following the principles of elemental absorption, intentions can be imparted into the food and drink you consume and the air you breathe. This is like blessing them with the energy of intention. The following practices will help attune your energy body to your intentions. This will flow into your physical body and have positive effects. This also helps engage your higher self and the universal law of attraction, to energize and attract what you focus upon into your body and your life.

Breathing with Intention

Sit and relax, close your eyes, and center yourself. Begin observing yourself breathing, feeling yourself taking air into your lungs. Focus on the leading edge of each breath and feel this moving through your nose and down into and filling your lungs. As you do this, fill your mind with a single intention and feel yourself breathing in this intention with each breath. Your intention might be health, vitality, healing, wisdom, happiness, luck, or wealth. Continue for ten breaths or more. Concentrate during this time and do not allow any other thoughts to enter your mind. Focus solely on absorbing your intention. Feel the intention being absorbed into your body with each breath. Use only one intention at a time and do not mix intentions during a session.

Intentionalizing Food and Drink

Before you eat or drink, take a moment to relax and center yourself. Formulate a single intention like health, vitality, healing, wisdom, happiness, luck, or wealth. State the intention in your mind and imagine and feel your energy and intention flowing into your food or drink, as if you are giving these healing. Continue for ten seconds or more.

The above method can be enhanced with a simple body awareness action. Focus on your intention, and on the *in* breath pull energy up through your legs and torso to your heart. Then, as you breathe *out*, push the energy out through your arms and hands and into your food and drink. Repeat your intention several times in your mind as you are breathing it out. Continue for several breaths or more.

Take your time on this exercise. Concentrate and hold your intention clear while you are energizing and imparting your intention. Eat and drink slowly, consciously, and thoughtfully. Get involved with what you are consuming. Be aware that you are ingesting your intention. Consume everything that you have energized. If something is thrown away, this demonstrates to your higher self that you do not want all of what your intention implies. However, it is okay to leave part of your meal and eat it later, or to give it to another person.

Energy Tools

Energy tools are thought form constructs that add purposeful intention to energy work actions. This enhances the effects of energy work for specific purposes. For example, if you want to burn away a tumor or an energy blockage, instead of using body awareness actions alone, you can imagine and intend a blowtorch to burn it away. If you want to cool inflammation, you can imagine a hose spraying water. Color and elements can also be added to energy work actions in this way.

The more often energy tools are used and the more energy is put into them, the more effective they become. The intention used imparts function to the energetic action. Intention can be love, compassion, healing, or to relax, cheer, revitalize, burn away disease, remove energy blockages, ease suffering or grief, cool a hot temper, and so on.

The following sections describe a range of useful energy work tools. More complex tools can be created as necessary. We will be using these energy tools more in the book ahead.

Disposal Fire

The disposal fire is an imagined and intended toxic energy disposal device. Its function is to automatically capture and incinerate anything you throw in its direction. This furnace follows you around and is always available. For example, imagine throwing a lump of toxic energy into the fire with the intention that it will be incinerated.

The fire responds by catching the toxic energy and flaring with intense heat as the lump is destroyed. A disposal device can be a simple bonfire, a miniature sun, or even a plasma incinerator with an automatic lid.

At the start of each session where energy tools will be used, imagine the disposal fire close to you as strongly and clearly as you can. As you do this, state its purpose three times or more in your mind with the command, "This fire destroys toxic energy." Imagine and feel your energy flowing into your disposal fire and making it hot and effective.

Golden Net and Sieve

The golden net is used to filter and remove particles and lumps of toxic energy and disease. Imagine and feel you are holding a golden net with a fine mesh.

At the start of each session, imagine holding the golden net in your body awareness hand. Hold up the net in front of you and imagine it as strongly and clearly as you can. As you do this, state its purpose three times or more in your mind with the command, "My golden net catches toxic energy." Imagine and feel your energy flowing into the net and making it effective and real.

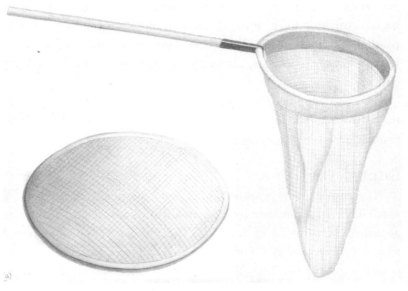

Move the net through your body one limb or body part at a time. Adjust the size of the net as necessary. Imagine and feel the net filtering and catching particles and lumps of toxic energy. Work your way through your whole body. Then enlarge the golden net and pass it over and through your entire body, scooping from your feet to your head. After each pass, dump the net's contents into your disposal fire. Either empty the net into the fire or throw in the whole net and instantly create another. Each net dump should only take a second or two. Repeat as necessary.

A circular sieve is a useful variation if the golden net does not fit certain tasks. A sieve can also be composed of sticky thread or absorbent cloth so it can be moved back and forth through the body with the intention of picking up sticky bits and toxic energy stains.

Flaming Torch

The flaming torch has many uses. Its flame can be large or small, widespread or tightly focused. This tool is used to burn away damaged or diseased parts of the physical body and to burn away energy blockages, lumps of toxic energy, and thick, sluggish energy. The flaming torch is also an excellent way to apply the fire element.

At the start of each session, imagine holding the flaming torch in your body awareness hand. Hold it in front of you and imagine it as strongly and clearly as you can. As you do this, state its purpose three times or more in your mind with the command, "My flaming torch burns away disease and toxic energy." Imagine and feel your energy flowing into the torch, making it effective and real.

When you use the flaming torch, imagine it igniting and the flame adjusting to the size and intensity you want. Apply this to the body part or organ you wish to work on or to the person you are healing. Imagine the flame burning away only diseased or damaged material. Healthy tissue remains unharmed. If you wish to burn away a tumor or damaged bone, you would imagine and intend the flame to be burning away only this. Imagine smoke and ash appearing as the damaged parts are destroyed. Finish the process with a few passes with your golden net or sieve to pick up any toxic residue.

Spray Gun

The spray gun is used to cool, clean, soothe, and restore damaged areas and to wash away toxic energy. It sprays water, foam, and other healing fluids.

At the start of each session, imagine holding the spray gun in your body awareness hand. Imagine holding this in front of you as strongly and clearly as you can. As you do this, state its purpose three times or more in your mind with the command, "My spray gun cools and cleans and restores." Imagine and feel your energy flowing into the spray gun and making it effective and real.

To repair a damaged area of the spine, first burn away the damaged bone, disk, and scar tissue with the flaming torch, and then

scoop away the residue with the golden net. Then apply a heavy, drenching spray of cool water to reduce inflammation. Finish by applying lots of pastel blue healing foam. Imagine pale-blue foam gushing from the spray gun, building up like mounds of shaving foam, and then sinking into and rebuilding the damaged area. Finish by imagining the damaged area as being perfect, strong, and healthy. As you do this, say three times or more in your mind, "This spine is strong and healthy."

The spray gun can also be used to apply the water element or mixtures of elements. For example, imagining a wet mist combines water and air, hot water combines fire and water, superheated steam combines fire and water and air, and molten lava combines earth, fire, and water. Other variations can be made by applying logic to the elemental analogy mixture.

Brilliant Fluid

Brilliant fluid is a penetrating tool that is used to add concentrated, positive energy to any area of the body. This helps to penetrate damaged areas, diseased tissue and bone, and toxic energy nodules.

Brilliant fluid can also be used to apply elements, including the water element and white-hot lava.

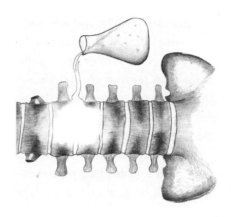

At the start of each session, imagine and feel yourself holding a flask of brilliant fluid in your body awareness hand. Hold this up and imagine its blinding brilliance as strongly and clearly as you can. As you do this, state its purpose three times or more in your mind with the command, "My brilliant fluid penetrates and restores." Imagine and feel your energy flowing into the fluid and making it brilliant and effective.

To use this tool, imagine and feel yourself pouring brilliant fluid into the area you are working upon, say a knee joint. Imagine the fluid soaking into and penetrating deeply into the joint, making it glow brightly. Then imagine the knee joint as being perfect and strong. As you do this, three times or more in your mind say, "This knee joint is healthy and perfect."

Energy Needles

Energy needles are deep penetration tools. These are inserted into areas of the body to reach deeper layers of damage and to pierce and weaken stubborn energy blockages and toxic nodules from the inside.

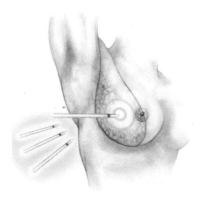

At the start of each session, imagine yourself holding a handful of brilliant energy needles, each the length of a pencil, in one body awareness hand. Imagine their brilliance as strongly and clearly as you can. As you do this, state their purpose three times or more in your mind with the command, "My energy needles are sharp and penetrating." Imagine and feel your energy flowing into the needles, making them bright and effective.

To use this tool, imagine you have an infinite supply of sharp, brilliant energy needles in one hand. These are highly charged and glittering with positive energy. Take a needle with your other awareness hand and push it deep into the area you are working upon. Imagine the needles glowing brightly and feel them penetrating as you insert them one at a time.

Energy needles can also be imagined as being hollow so that brilliant fluid and healing elements can be blasted though them deep into damaged areas and hard blockages. A hypodermic syringe can also be created and used for this purpose.

Iron Pincers

Iron pincers are heavy-duty tools that are used to rip out chunks of toxic energy, tumors, and diseased tissue. They are incinerated in the disposal fire.

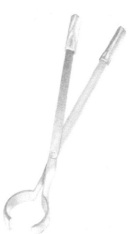

At the start of each session, imagine and feel yourself holding the pincers in your body awareness hands. Imagine holding these in front of you as strongly and clearly as you can. As you do this, state their purpose three times or more in your mind with the command, "My iron pincers remove toxic lumps." Imagine and feel your energy flowing into the pincers and making them effective and real.

To use this tool, imagine and feel yourself holding the iron pincers. Adjust the size as necessary. Push them into the area you are working upon and feel yourself clamping shut the jaws. Then imagine yourself ripping the lump out of your body and tossing it into your disposal fire. Repeat as necessary.

The more time and effort put into imagining and using energy tools, the more effective they will become. This can be time-consuming, but it is an effective method for removing toxic energy and repairing diseased areas of the body. These procedures are equally as effective for self-healing as for healing others.

Atmosphere Cleansing and Shielding

The plank technique given earlier can be used outside of the physical body to clear toxic atmospheres and create energy barriers and personal shielding. This will help if you feel invaded or impinged upon by exterior negative energies and intentions. This could happen in a shopping mall, during or after a confrontation, or for no discernable reason whatsoever. It is wise to learn and practice these methods in case you ever have need of them.

The first step is to start a full body–length plank action, spinning it clockwise around yourself close to your skin, as we did earlier. Increase the speed of the action and imagine it whooshing around you as the plank speeds up and swings further out. Adjust the speed and distance until your plank is spinning around you about six feet (two meters) out.

When your plank action is steady, focus on the inside area of the plank action around you and mentally or verbally repeat several times the command, "I cleanse this space of all negative beings and toxic energy." Next, imagine that the plank is connected to your body with a sheet of brilliant light the length of your whole body. Imagine the plank spinning around you and the brilliant cloth cleansing everything it touches inside its perimeter. Repeat the command as necessary.

Commands and affirmations are far more powerful when spoken verbally. Your throat primary center will empower everything you say out loud, projecting your voice into subtle dimensions around you.

To create an energy shield, continue the above plank and light sheet actions. Imagine and feel the brilliant, light cloth wrapping around you and building up layer upon layer of thick and impenetrable white light shielding. Imagine and feel this building up over the full length of your body. Mentally or verbally say three times or more the command, "This shield is impenetrable." Continue for as long as necessary. With practice, this method can be done anywhere and in any position: standing, sitting, or lying down.

The above shielding method can also contain elemental properties. It is best to absorb the elements being used first. This can be done fairly quickly. A shield can be composed of fire or white-hot lava. Earth and rock or water can be added by projecting these into the shield. Iron shielding can be added with imagination and intention. Pure white light can also be added to water, like the brilliant fluid given earlier. A command should be used to reinforce your shield's intention. Mentally or verbally repeat several times something like, "This shield repels all negative beings and forces."

Caution: It is unwise to use too large a plank action in disturbed areas, haunted houses, et cetera. This can stimulate and provoke unwanted attention from discarnate entities and forces in the area. The idea is to create a clean, shielded personal space around yourself.

Group Plank Work

Plank action stimulation and shielding can be adapted for group work. This can be used for connecting a group energetically and for cleansing and shielding a group area. To perform this kind of group work, all members should first practice the plank action individually. Anyone can do a plank action with a little instruction.

Group Circle Method

To begin, have the group sit in a circle. Hold hands or not; it makes no difference. Place candles or flowers in the middle of the circle to create a central point of reference. Begin your group session in your usual way. Have the group relax, and then begin a joint plank action spinning clockwise through the whole circle, *through* all of the group members. Each group member pushes the plank action to their left, through all other group members in the circle, and then back through themselves in a continuous clockwise plank action. Continue this for a minute or so.

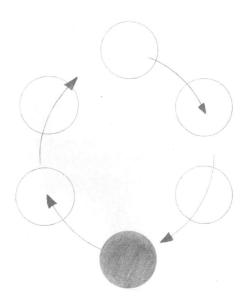

Plank Action Timing

With a group circle of 10 feet in diameter, the plank action should be about two to four seconds per circuit. This action does not have to be synchronized. Some members will be faster or slower; everyone should go at their own best pace. Everyone contributes to the group energy dynamic being created.

Group Cleansing

To cleanse the group area, have everyone perform individual plank actions, with the radius of each person's plank action almost touching the person opposite. Have members imagine that their planks are trailing sheets of brilliant white light, as we did earlier with the atmosphere-cleansing method. Then have the group mentally or verbally make the following command several

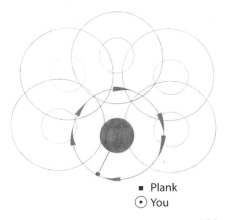

■ Plank
⊙ You

times: "I cleanse this space of all negative beings and forces." Continue for a minute or two.

Group Shielding

Have the group perform a slightly faster plank action so that all plank actions are moving around just *outside* the group perimeter (rather than through everyone). Continue for a minute, until everyone is settled. Then have the group imagine that their planks are trailing

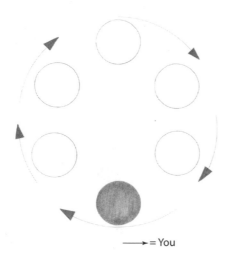

→ = You

wide sheets of thick, brilliant white energy. Have the group imagine these energy sheets building up layer upon layer of thick, white light and creating a shell around the group. Then have the group mentally or verbally make the following command several times: "This shield is impenetrable to negative beings and forces." Continue for a minute or two.

Elemental Shielding

To add simple elemental shielding to the above, first familiarize the group with the practice of absorbing elements, as given earlier. Then have the group start a plank and sheet of light shielding action around the group, as we did above. Have the group imagine their planks' sheets of light as being made of fire. This forms an elemental shield around the outside of the group. Continue for two minutes or more. Once the shield is in place, all group members should make the following command mentally or verbally several times: "This shield is impenetrable to negative beings and forces."

Spend a few minutes building and reinforcing these shields. They are an effective means of cleansing and shielding a person or group.

Composite Shielding

More elaborate shields can be built by mixing elements with imagination and intent. A shield of white-hot lava, for example, contains fire, water, and earth. Each group member can be given a separate color, element, or substance (for example, fire, water, earth air, rock, brick, et cetera) to add to the group shield to form a composite shield.

The shield height is unimportant. The easiest height to perform a plank action is head high, sitting or standing. It is more difficult to do this at ceiling level or above. Also, in my experience, all negative spirit entities are bound to the surface of the earth. They are essentially two dimensional beings, and as such, they cannot fly over this type of energy barrier. For more information on these matters see my book *Practical Psychic Self-Defense: Understanding and Surviving Unseen Influences* (Hampton Roads, 2002).

Caution: This type of group energy work can make some people nauseous, particularly if they are not used to body awareness energy work. This is a natural reaction to strong group energy passing through sensitive individuals. This is rarely more than a minor and temporary problem. If this happens, though, the group should take a short break before continuing. Repeat this break, if necessary, until everyone is comfortable with this level of energy work.

Grounding

Body awareness energy work practices have the effect of waking up many aspects of the energy body and spiritual consciousness from dormancy. Sometimes this can cause imbalances and over-activity in energy centers, which can cause a variety of problems. Some people can become elementally, energetically, and even psychologically unbalanced or ungrounded. Symptoms can include anxiety, depression, mood swings, lethargy, hyperactivity, ebullience, disassociation, and feelings of being scattered and disconnected from life.

Energy imbalances affect some people more than others and in varying degrees. The average person is naturally well grounded and energetically robust. But even grounded people can experience imbalance problems at times, especially when undertaking high levels of energy work and spiritual practice.

A popular misconception involves a one-sided view of spiritual energies. Modern New Age people tend to stimulate and attract mainly higher spiritual energies. But to function well on all levels, like having a balanced diet and exercising regularly, we need a balanced intake of energies. Low vibration energies are not negative or toxic or bad, any more than are low musical notes and tones. Negative and toxic energies are *disharmonious*, and it is this disharmony that makes them unhealthy. Low vibrational energies are grounding, balancing, and healthy, and should be an essential part of one's elemental dietary balance.

A second popular misconception is that low vibrational energies should be avoided. This can lead to overstimulation of higher primary centers, the exclusion of lower primary center stimulation, and low vibrational frequency energy absorption. In the modern world, this often leads to overstimulation of the brow and crown centers. These tendencies come in part from translated Eastern sources of esoteric knowledge that were brought to the West over the past two centuries.

I am in no way criticizing Eastern traditions here, but it should be kept in mind that ancient sources of knowledge sprang largely from heavily grounded agricultural societies. In those days, people were more in touch with the land. By and large, they lived simpler and more grounded lives than we do today. Stimulating the higher energy centers of such heavily grounded people would not cause the problems that it does today. Compared to this, we live in a fast-paced, modern world that is highly stimulating to the mind and senses. This includes the media (TV, music, computers, games, books, et cetera) and the types of work people do today.

Modern life is complex and mentally overstimulating to the point where many people struggle to cope with the massive onslaught of information. We of the modern world live largely in our minds, in a complex knowledge- and information-based age. This overstimulation of the mind overstimulates the higher primary energy centers.

Given this, it is obviously unwise to further overstimulate the higher primary centers without giving thought to balancing ourselves. We must account for and deal with the higher energies that modern life produces in us by default. This is part of the reason why the energy work taught in this book starts from the ground up and encourages a balanced approach to energetic development.

Two basic functions of primary energy centers are to *transform* and *accumulate* energy. Stimulating the higher primary centers causes increased absorption of high vibrational energies. This can be countered by working more on the lower primary centers and by drawing in more of the heavier earth and water elements. It is healthiest to pull the earth element into the lower primary centers, the base and the navel, since these are attuned to this vibration of energy. But in cases of major imbalances where people feel scattered, dizzy, or even manic and psychotic, pouring the earth element directly into the head area and the brow and crown centers for a short time can be very grounding and healing.

The good news here is that energy imbalances can be rectified by elemental absorption and grounding practices. With these simple methods, it is possible to flood the energy body with the heavier, low vibration energies. The accumulation and absorption of earth and water elements given earlier is an excellent way to counter excesses of high vibrational energy and balance overactive higher primary centers.

Listening to deep tones and voices—like Zen or Gregorian chanting, baritone singers, and other low vibrational sounds and music—can help one absorb low vibrational grounding energies more easily.

Energetic imbalance is an increasing problem in the modern world. This is particularly noticeable in our children. The massive rise in ADHD (Attention Deficit Hyperactivity Disorder) and other such disorders of mind and personality are, I think, symptomatic of a mentally overstimulated world. Elemental imbalance appears to be a significant part of this problem. The earth element is traditionally not added to the head area because it slows mental processes. In our modern world, though, there are exceptions where this can be healing. For an overstimulated mind and body, the earth element will always have a calming effect.

Other Grounding Methods

There are a number of other grounding methods that help deactivate the energy body and help reduce problems related to excessive higher energies.

Taking a Break

This is the first thing to do if you develop symptoms of energetic imbalance. Cease all energy work and spiritual practices, including meditation. Focus exclusively on physical life. This is a time to catch up on real life, to fix things that have been put off, to do gardening, to visit friends, to engage in social activities, or to swim, shop, cook, walk, play golf, or go fishing. In particular, try to do heavy grounding things like mowing the lawn and gardening. Smell the grass; get your hands dirty and *earthy*. While doing this, avoid spiritual thoughts and put all of your effort into engaging *fully* with life and connecting with the earth.

Earth Energy Dump

A simple grounding method is to lie on the ground and perform an energy dump. Imagine thick cords extending from all of your primary centers down into the earth. Take your time so you can imagine and feel this well. Imagine and feel yourself connecting with the heavy, molten gravity center of the earth. Feel the gravity pulling and making you feel heavier and heavier. Imagine and feel your excess higher energies being pulled from you and flowing into the earth. Say the words, mentally or verbally, "I give my energy to the Earth." Take your time and let your excess energy drain away.

Next, still lying on the ground, imagine and feel the heavy substance of the earth pumping up the cords and filling your body with its lead-like, molten heaviness. Breathe this in and feel it soaking into your body. Feel yourself growing heavier and heavier. Relax and take your time.

Shower Energy Dump

Take a shower and imagine and feel your excess energy flowing out of your body and being washed away by the water. Feel the water running down over your skin with your body awareness senses. Imagine and feel this is draining your body of excess energy.

Salt Bath Energy Dump

Salt is a crystal with the ability to absorb energy. Draw a warm bath and add a few pounds of cheap rock salt or sea salt. Make sure you are properly hydrated and that you have drinking water on hand before taking a heavy salt bath, as this can cause dehydration. (If in doubt of your ability to take a heavy salt bath, check with your doctor.) Soak in the bath for one hour or more. Add more warm water as necessary. Then drain it while you are still lying in the bath. Feel the water level lowering. Feel all of your excess energy being sucked from your body by the water as it drains. Focus intently on this action with your body awareness senses. Then take a cool shower to remove excess salt from your skin. This is an effective way of removing not only excess energy, but also accumulations of negative and toxic energy. Repeat this one or two days apart, as necessary. (Not suitable for septic fields.)

Running Water Energy Dump

A running water energy dump can be performed just about anywhere. Running water grounds the electromagnetic properties of the energy body. This drains excess energy and toxic energy, and helps restore balance. This method can be done in the shower or by standing over coils of garden hose gushing water, standing on a bridge or next to a creek or river, or standing above an underground water supply main pipe. (This method will also quickly stop psychic or negative entity interference.)

Stand over or above running water, close your eyes, and take a few deep breaths to settle yourself. Imagine dazzling light pouring into your head like a thick, luminous fluid. Concentrate and imagine this fluid filling your head and then your chest, stomach, and legs. As you do this, also imagine and feel discolored fluid pouring out of your feet and washing or soaking away. Continue for a few minutes or for as long as necessary.

Eating and Sleeping

When all else fails, eat. Preparing and cooking food is very grounding. Take some time out to eat good meals—and to catch up on your sleep. Heavy protein is particularly good for shutting down the energy body. A sleep deficit will tend to stimulate the higher centers, which will compound energetic overactivity problems. Eating and catching up on your sleep will help restore balance. This will not remove excess energy per se, but it will slow and ground your energy body.

Practice

Perform the physical relaxation exercise, and then relax yourself with awareness breathing. Pre-stimulate your hands and arms, and your feet and legs. Perform a whole body energy bounce using large, colored energy balls. Start with red, and then orange, yellow, green, blue, purple, violet, and brilliant white. Perform the full body circuit for a few minutes until well settled. Then spend a few minutes relaxing your body and mind more deeply with awareness breathing.

Imagine each of the energy tools in turn: the disposal fire, golden net and sieve, flaming torch, spray gun, brilliant fluid, energy needles, and iron pincers. Imagine these one at a time and mentally or verbally state each tool's intention command three times.

Target an area of your body that needs repair and work on it with each of the energy tools. Take your time over this. If you have no areas needing repair, work on your lower spine.

- Practice the elemental absorption method with fire, water, air, and earth.
- Impart a vitality intention into a glass of water and drink it consciously.
- Practice the plank and sheet of light cleansing and shielding methods.
- Lie on the floor or grass and practice the grounding and energy dump methods.

We have discussed ways of charging energy actions and constructs with imagination and intention, absorbing elements, creating energy tools, and grounding. Coming up next, we take a closer look at energy blockages and how to go about clearing them.

SIX

Energy Blockages

This chapter discusses the nature of energy blockages and how to identify and repair blocked, sluggish, and damaged areas of your energy body. Removing and healing these areas is a significant part of spiritual development work.

The human energy body can be likened to a river system flowing from the mountains to the ocean. Over time, changes in the land affect the rivers and streams and enforce changes. These changes sometimes cause waterways to become blocked or silted up in parts. Fast-flowing rivers spread out into myriad streams, wetlands, and swamps, and then recombine into rivers. Clean water becomes muddy, garbage accumulates, and oxbows and islands form. Sometimes, although we notice reduced water flow, the events responsible happened so long ago or are so far upstream that we cannot see them clearly and identify the causative factors.

As you progress with energetic and spiritual development work, you will become steadily more in tune with your energy body. The more you work with energy, the more layers and finer internal structures you will perceive. You may discover energy blockages now or later. Everyone has them in some way, shape, or form.

There are many reasons why sluggish, stuck, or dysfunctional areas appear in the energy body. There is a direct relationship between the physical body, the mind, and the energy body. When we are born, our energy bodies are usually vibrant and full of life. But as we age, we learn to suppress our natural emotional guidance system and intuitive feelings. We accumulate beliefs, programming, traumas, core hurts, and physical damage. These often result in blocked, dysfunctional, or inactive areas of the energy body, and in disease. It is often difficult to look back and clearly identify the causes of core hurts and the energy blockages they produce. Discovering these things is a serious part of spiritual development work and of one's growth as a person.

Most energy blockages involving core hurts will respond to a psychological approach, resolving issues and coming to terms with past events and present-life conditions. Direct body awareness energy work is another approach to the same thing. This targets nodes of stuck energy that are at the heart of core hurts.

Considerable evidence suggests that the subconscious mind overlays the physical body, which indicates that the memories relating to core hurts are actually located in parts of the physical body. And this is my experience. Occasionally, energy work triggers specific memories and emotions, and the memory of an event surfaces with its full emotional content as if it had only just happened. This often causes powerful emotional releases. The memories involved often have been completely forgotten before this moment. The actions most likely to cause such releases involve work on primary energy centers.

Core hurts can also be described as core images, or thought form cysts. Their existence creates enduring nodules of disharmonious energy in the energy body. These are composed of dense, negative thoughts and memories and *stuck* energies relating to unresolved conflicts, traumas, and core hurts. These can manifest a whole spectrum of diseases and disorders. Core hurts can be treated with body awareness energy work methods, as well as by psychotherapy. A joint approach is by far the most effective.

In the case of physical disease, the site of an energy blockage will usually be evident and manifest as a diseased or dysfunctional organ or body part. Once something like this is identified, it can be targeted and worked on with body awareness actions, intention, and energy tools. In the case of psychological problems, the actual site of energy cysts and blockages may not be apparent. These, however, will often be uncovered in time through energy work practice as deeper layers and structures of the energy body are revealed.

Blockages will often involve body parts where there is densification in the energy body due to toxic energy accumulation, physical and emotional traumas, a body part that is not loved, negative thoughts and beliefs regarding life, suppressed or blocked emotions, low self-esteem, anger, or guilt, or lack of self-worth and self-love. A healthy sense of whole body and whole person self-love, in particular, is paramount to long-term health and well-being. It is also necessary for significant spiritual development and growth as a person.

Spirit entity attachments can also cause or be connected to energy cysts and blockages. Typically, negative spirit entities attach to trauma memories, core hurts, and weaknesses in the human psyche and memory. The methods given in this book will help heal these, but this is a specialized subject beyond the scope of this book. For further reading on these matters, and for dealing with psychic attack, negative spirit beings and attachments, I recommend my book: *Practical Psychic Self-Defense: Understanding and Surviving Unseen Influences* (Hampton Roads, 2002).

A variety of symptoms can indicate energy blockages and cysts. Some will only become apparent during or after energy work. This is because energy work increases one's energy body sensitivity and awareness. Energy work will typically produce mild warmth, tingling, and slight heaviness in the area on which you are working. Stronger sensations are common for early energy work, but these should progressively reduce to comfortable levels. Anything out of the ordinary can indicate problems. You may feel no sensations in an area, an area may feel thicker or sluggish or just different, or you may feel stronger sensations in or pain when you move body awareness through an area. All of these things can indicate that some kind of energy body problem or blockage may exist.

Physical Symptoms

The most noticeable symptoms caused by touching core hurt–related energy cysts and blockage with body awareness energy work actions are emotional releases and the flash recovery of memories. But a range of physical symptoms can manifest through the practice of energy work.

The physical body and its energy body are intimately connected. What affects one affects the other. Occasional reactions to body awareness energy work are energy rashes and lumps. These are primarily caused by overstimulation of sluggish or inactive areas of the energy body. The physical body's nerves are affected by this, which can cause temporary skin blemishes to appear. These can look like any other rash or lump, ranging from red blotches and spots to small, watery blisters on the skin to swollen lumps like hives or insect bites. These will usually disappear within a day or two, often within hours, as the physical body adapts to the increased bioenergic flow.

While uncommon, more severe reactions to intensive energy work on energy cysts and blockages are localized physical infections. Energy work generally stimulates a healing response in the physical body. However, some energy cysts and blockages seem to contain such large amounts of negative energy that, when disturbed, physical infection can result. If symptoms of infection, redness, swelling, and pain arise in an area on which you have been intensively working, please seek medical attention.

I have experienced several minor and two major infections resulting from energy work to clear cysts and blockages. Of the two serious infections, one was located in my coccyx and the other in my right elbow joint. Neither began with broken skin or any other identifiable cause—my doctor and the specialists I saw were mystified. At these times I was aware of energy blockages in these areas and had been doing intensive energy work upon them, experimenting with ways to remove them. Both infections began with localized redness and swelling that soon became painful. Fortunately, I connected the symptoms to the energy work I had been doing and sought medical attention early. Both infections were serious and required multiple courses of strong antibiotics to heal. The elbow joint infection caused blood poisoning and required a week of hospitalization and intravenous antibiotics. As said, please seek medical attention early if you develop any sign of infection.

Things That Help

The skin is the largest organ of the physical body. This is subtly represented by the outer layer of the egg-shaped aura of the energy body. The surface of the skin is covered with an intricate network of energy meridians and energy pores. The condition of the skin affects the flow of this surface energy, which in turn affects the whole energy body.

Skin likes air. Bare, well-cared-for skin provides optimal conditions for a healthy, natural flow of energy. Loose, clean clothing made of natural fibers like cotton and open shoes are the next best thing. (Synthetic fibers can interfere with energy flow.) Keeping the hands and feet free of calluses and thickened skin and keeping the nails clean and trimmed also help. These areas are the major conduits into the energy body, and extra care will improve energy flow. Podiatry and reflexology treatments will help improve energy flow through the feet, as will an extra change of socks each day and comfortable shoes.

The use of good-quality scented soaps, shampoos, and essential oils will also help improve energy flow in your skin. The application of essential oils directly to skin areas over known blockages can also be beneficial.

Extra Energy Cleaning Tools

Regular energy work on blockages will help restore energy flow. Some blockages are stubborn, though, and require significant work over time with heavy-duty energy tools to wear them down. Blockages and nodes related to core hurts and suppressed trauma memories can recur. Regular energy work is an excellent way of bringing these things to the surface so they can be processed and healed.

Imagination has no bounds. Any kind of energy tool you can imagine can be created and used with good effect. A fire hose, scrapers, chisels, wire brushes, electric drills, grinders, saws, jackhammers, and even explosives can be created and used. Created tools come with inherent intentions that are associated with their real-world functions. A power drill penetrates, a power grinder grinds, a vacuum cleaner sucks, dynamite explodes, and so on.

When using these extra tools, imagine the sound and action of the tool you are using, and imagine and feel the effect it is having upon the area on which you are working. For example, when using a mini jackhammer, imagine the hammering sound and feel it digging into the area you are working upon. Imagine and feel the energy blockage disintegrating, with bits and pieces flying off and dust and smoke appearing, et cetera. Adjust the size of energy tools to suit the application.

Clearing Blockages

There are many different types of energy blockages, and they all feel different. Some will be obvious and quickly identified. Others will not become apparent until energy work has been practiced for some time; that is, as you become more sensitized to the deeper layers of your energy body.

The fundamental principle of treating any energy blockage is to *pay it a lot of attention*. To begin with, energy balls should be repeatedly moved or bounced through the suspected area for a few minutes during each session. This is usually enough to awaken inactive areas and clear simple blockages, although multiple sessions may still be required. Vary the actions and use the energy tools introduced earlier, plus create any other energy tools you feel are suited to your purpose.

The length of time it takes to clear an energy blockage or cyst varies greatly. Some will respond in a few sessions, but some can take weeks, months, or even years before they are properly cleared. Often, an energy node or blockage will appear to succumb when only one layer of it has been removed. As said, a blockage may resurface in the same area if the underlying causes—especially hidden psychological core hurts at the roots of energy blockages—have not been healed.

Detailed Hand and Foot Work

Extra hand and foot work helps clear energy blockages not only in the hands and feet, but also in the entire energy body. Energy that flows into the energy body through the hands and feet streams into the meridian system. If you have blockages in the hands and feet, energy flowing into the meridians is changed, reduced, or hampered. This affects the functioning of all associated biological processes and organs. Energy must be able to flow freely through the energy body for optimal health.

The body awareness brushing action given earlier can be used on each side of every finger and toe: top and bottom, left and right. The stirring and wrapping actions can be used on every finger and toe joint. This practice takes time, but the increased energy flow makes it time well spent.

Energy cysts and blockages can feel like small dense spots or little pebbles and lumps in the substance of the energy body to your body awareness senses. These can occur anywhere. If you move awareness intensely back and forth through such an area, you may feel small spots that you cannot easily penetrate. More intensive energy work on such areas may cause sharp pains, or you may feel nothing but peculiar numb sensations.

Tracking down energy cysts and blockages requires experimentation and observation. Carry out intensive energy work on suspect areas and observe how they feel when they respond. Work your way through your body one part at a time. If there are no clear indications of blockages anywhere, start with your feet. Start with your toes one at a time, and then work your way up through each foot joint and bone, ankle, calf muscle, knee joint, et cetera. If you do not discover anything, this exploratory work will still be beneficial as it improves general energy flow in your body.

Calluses occur naturally as skin thickens in response to repeated friction. Unusual calluses and hard tissue that are not caused by friction can indicate deep-seated energy blockages. This could involve rough or thickened patches of skin on an elbow, knee, thumb, or anywhere on your body. Note anything unusual and explore it with extra energy work attention.

Intensive Foot Work Example

A good way to clear deep energy blockages is to use highly focused body awareness brushing actions along energy pathways and meridians. Using energy tools like stiff wire brushes, scrapers, and needles also helps. The energy lines in the diagrams coming up can only be felt while using tightly focused penetrating, brushing, and scraping actions in those areas. These would not usually be felt during normal levels of energy work.

The heavy, sluggish energy mentioned below is commonly associated with long-term inactive areas of the energy body. This can coat any part of the body, but it is usually much thicker when found in the feet. Body awareness energy work will progressively clear away sluggish energy, but more intensive attention will help clear thicker areas more quickly. This is also necessary to perceive hidden energy cysts and nodes.

The feet are the major conduits into the energy body. This is where energy is exchanged with the planet. Toxic energies drain from and fresh energies flow into the energy body there. Blockages in this area will not only slow the intake of healthy energies, but also cause accumulations of toxic energies in the body. The importance of keeping the feet physically and energetically clear and healthy cannot be overemphasized.

The following case history is from an advanced energy worker. This is typical of treating deep-seated blockages and cysts with energy tools. (The bubbling well point produces a bubbling water sensation when active.)

Deep calluses grew in the middle of my soles for no physical reason during my teens. These sometimes made walking painful, like there were stones in my shoes. These calluses are directly in the bubbling well points. [Taoist term for the middle area behind the toes that dents when a foot is pointed.] I recently targeted these areas because they seemed likely to contain energy blockages.

When I first started working intensively on my feet, I felt lots of heavy, sluggish energy coating them. This felt to be about one inch thick to my body awareness sense. My first task was, obviously, to break this away so I could get at what was beneath. My left foot was more difficult to work on and took longer than my right foot. It took several long sessions before I made a breakthrough, where I succeeded in punching a hole through the sluggish energy of one foot. This breakthrough produced very strong energy sensations. Once this was done, I worked on widening the hole. I then started to perceive the energy lines and structures in my feet more clearly. I repeated this procedure on my other foot. It was almost like I had to tear my way through thick, armor-like energy skin in order to connect with the deeper and finer energetic structures within my feet.

The feet contain complex energy structures and configurations of energy lines. Lines run from all toes to the heels. Two larger energy lines run from the second and third toes and pass through the bubbling well points. I feel a scattering of small, hard energy nodes in all the lines in my feet, but the main concentrations are in the bubbling well points.

I brush the energy lines that go through the bubbling well point on all sides. I can feel small, hard lumps there. When I penetrate and break up a lump, I feel a bubbling, burning, tingling energy flow moving to my heel. At this point, I often feel a sharp pain either in a big toe or a heel. If I break several nodes during a session, my calves and feet feel bruised and strained; it can be difficult to walk first thing next morning. Leg stretching and massage helps with this.

The energy tools I use are a small,

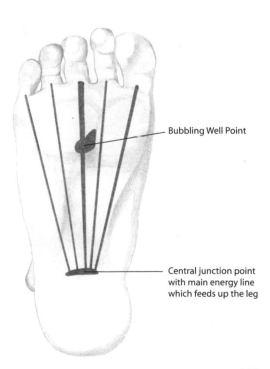

Bubbling Well Point

Central junction point with main energy line which feeds up the leg

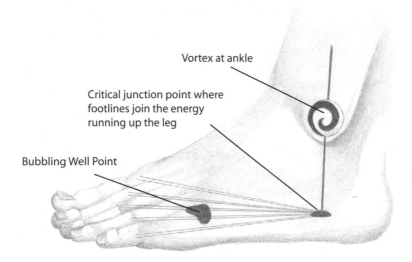

Vortex at ankle

Critical junction point where
footlines join the energy
running up the leg

Bubbling Well Point

visualized hard-wire brush, a chisel of light and hammer, a
scraper, and brilliant-light hollow needles. Part of the problem
with dense energy nodes is penetrating them. When I work on
a node with a wire brush energy tool, it can take 20 minutes or
more of hard, focused work to break it apart. When I use a
hammer and chisel of light, the chisel often slides off the node
and does not connect well. Energy needles are the best tool I
have found to penetrate hard nodes. I insert several hollow
needles into the node and blast brilliant, light energy through
the needles. This action seems to shatter the nodes from the
inside.

Intensive fine energy work is best learned by first working
on the hands (before working on the feet). This is because it is
easier to focus fine awareness actions in the hands. Create a
small, stiff wire brush and work on brushing the fingers and
energy lines in the hands. This teaches you how to get tightly
focused actions to penetrate. To intensify the force of this
action, progressively stiffen the wire bristles. Experiment with
using other fine energy tools.

Alternative Energy Work Methods

To remove widespread sluggish energy and/or to bring sluggish areas of the energy body out of dormancy, it can help to use alternative methods. Heavy-duty awareness actions and/or lengthy meditative energy work practice sessions can make all the difference. You should try both of the methods given below. Once sluggish energy is reduced and dormant areas are activated, your energy body will become more sensitized and responsive to body awareness actions. It will then respond better to normal levels of energy work and other spiritual practices.

Heavy-Duty Energy Work

Heavy-duty energy work is recommended as a temporary development measure. This will help people who are experiencing little or no energy-related sensations during practice sessions. Heavy energy balls can be bounced through any inactive part of the body, even primary centers, to stimulate them into activity. Sometimes it can take an hour or more to get in touch with and activate some areas of the energy body. Once a heavy action is settled into, energy body memory makes it relatively easy to continue for any length of time.

Heavy energy bounce actions work better if the body or body part being worked on is reasonably straight. There is a slight resistance and loss of awareness intensity and speed caused by bouncing heavy, rapid actions through bent joints. Straightening the body will help you get the most out of heavy energy work. This also applies to the spine and neck during whole body bounce actions. Heavy work is, therefore, best done while lying completely flat, with legs and arms reasonably straight. Even a slight elevation of the head caused by a pillow can interfere with heavy awareness bouncing through the neck. This resistance can be felt when a heavy bounce action is intensified. Some people find it helps to lie flat with their arms above their heads. Experiment and see what works best for you.

Long Session Meditative Energy Work

Long session meditative work can help activate sluggish and dormant areas of the energy body. Set aside a few hours when you will not be disturbed. Turn the lights down low. Relax and do awareness breathing to settle yourself. Pre-stimulate, use the full-body circuit, and stimulate each of your primary centers. Do the spinal, central channel, and whole body bounces for a few minutes each. Then relax and focus only on your feet. Move energy balls back and forth through them at a comfortable rate. Use awareness breathing to gently achieve a deeper state of relaxation. Continue relaxing and brushing your feet. Do nothing else for two hours or more.

If you need to move for comfort during any lengthy exercise, do so in a relaxed and dreamy way. Have a water bottle handy. If you need a comfort break, your relaxed state can be maintained by slitting your eyes, moving slowly, and keeping silent. If you get bored, repeat the primary center stimulation and practice other exercises like the plank and two tube methods for a short time, and then return to your feet. Take your time over this. Stay relaxed and let yourself really settle into this gentle practice.

After an hour-and-a-half or so into any deeply relaxed meditative practice, you will experience a subtle but profound change. This change relates to how the activity of your mind and your level of sleep consciousness would change after a similar time spent asleep. If everything goes well, you will find yourself in a profound mind awake/body asleep state (also called a trance state). Your energy body and its primary centers will become much more active in this state. The length of time spent stimulating your feet during this session will significantly increase whole body energy activity, including primary center activity.

Psychic and spiritual experiences and phenomena are more likely to occur in this relaxed state of consciousness. Brow center strobe episodes and clairvoyant experiences are also more likely to occur, as are awake lucid dreams and spontaneous astral projections.

Energy Blockage Release Issues

When energy body blockages are cleared, the end result is always improved energy flow—and sometimes the easement or healing of related disorders. This can involve physical, psychological, or spiritual problems.

Compressed emotional energy nodes resulting from traumatic real-life events are like energetic land mines. They are composed of tightly compressed, disharmonious emotions and memories. Clearing such a node can result in a powerful emotional release and even the return of suppressed memories, as discussed earlier. This is most common with blockages connected with primary energy centers, but the actual site of a compressed emotional memory node can be anywhere in the physical body. The actual physical size of such a node may only be that of a grain of sand.

I have experienced such emotional releases myself. I have also observed this happen to students while guiding them through energy work sessions. These are not uncommon events. Any body awareness energy work action can trigger these, but the most common trigger has been a body awareness slicing action.

Imagine a disk of shiny metal, like a pizza tray about 12 inches across, like the sieve introduced earlier. Starting at just below your buttocks, slide the disk side to side through your body. Raise this action a 16th of an inch (a few millimeters) at a time as you work your way up through your body to the top of your head. Imagine and feel this action passing side to side through your body. When you reach the top of your head, change the action to a back and forth action and slowly work your way back down to where you started. Take your time and focus on feeling the action moving through your body. This action can also be used on your arms and legs.

After an emotionally charged node is triggered, common side effects after the initial emotional release are feelings of emptiness and depression. This dark night of the soul can be devastating, but it is a temporary condition. It usually passes in a few days or so, depending on its power and content and how difficult it might be for you to process. This is an occasion to take some time out for yourself, to stop and sleep, think, and reflect. Give yourself whatever time and space you need to process what has been released. Give yourself time to grow into and fill the new empty space that may have appeared inside of you. In time, you will fill this with more of yourself. The end result is spiritual growth.

An emotionally charged energy node also occupies a subtle place in your consciousness. When released, this can be like uncovering and triggering the energy of a soul split, where a part of yourself, a snap-shot of yourself frozen in time, has broken away due to trauma. This frozen split-away part of yourself was created during the trauma. It has existed in that same moment ever since. Processing such a release will take time and work, and you may need help from others. Seek the help of loving psychologists and healers to help you work through and process this energy. Removing a powerful blockage, processing the causative event, and reintegrating the energy and consciousness involved back into yourself can be a painful but healing process.

Practice

Relax and center yourself with awareness breathing. Pre-stimulate your hands and arms, and your feet and legs. Complete a whole body bounce before starting the following exercises.

Focus awareness in your left foot. Work your way through it with a tightly focused awareness brushing action, imagining you are using a small, stiff, wire brush. Start with your toes and spend a few min-utes on each, digging in the brushing action and brushing as deeply as you can. Continue this, moving slowly and thoroughly, through the sole of your foot and heel, and then through the top of your foot. Try to feel the energy lines that pass through the bubbling well point with your body awareness senses. Practice using other awareness tools, wire brushes, chisels, scrapers, et cetera. Pay particular attention to any small, hard lumps you might feel with your senses. Repeat this exercise on your right foot.

Lie flat on your bed and use a heavy energy ball bounce on your arms and legs, one at a time. Then begin a large, whole body energy ball bounce. Imagine and feel this to be a heavy energy ball, as if full of water. Continue the whole body bounce for 10 minutes or more.

Focus on brushing both feet simultaneously with energy balls. Settle into this and continue for at least 20 minutes; the longer the better.

In this chapter, we have discussed ways of detecting and removing energy blockages. Coming up next, we look at how energy work can be used to heal yourself.

SEVEN

Self-Healing
with Energy

Any malady can be eased by shining the lights of consciousness and love upon its darkened shores. The knowledge and energy skills you have learned here can be used to generate healing energy for yourself, other people, and even animals. Anyone can generate a beneficial level of healing energy.

Under the right circumstances, the physical body can heal itself of just about anything. Energy work helps create these right circumstances. As said earlier, healers produce biomagnetic energy fields that trigger healing processes in their patients. This takes some of the magic out of healing, but this also makes healing more accessible. Some healers are gifted in this respect, but *everyone* is capable of producing a beneficial level of healing energy.

The self-healing process is empowered by taking interest in and being proactive about your physical condition. Your body cannot be replaced, so it is wise to look after it well. Seek medical opinion, research alternative treatments, and take your lifestyle, diet, and health seriously. If you take an interest in healing your physical self, your higher self will become interested in helping make this a reality.

Responsibility and Self-Love

From a spiritual perspective, it is beneficial to take responsibility for all of your life conditions, especially your health. Consciously, you may not have chosen things to be the way they are in your life, but at a higher spiritual level, you have done exactly that. This involves universal law: the law of attraction. The thoughts, images, programming, and beliefs in your mind continually engage your higher self. The law of attraction attracts things and events and life lessons to you according to the focus of your thoughts and beliefs. In this way, you create your own reality, including your state of health and all of your life's conditions and circumstances.

Giving away responsibility for your health and happiness confounds the self-healing process. Your higher spiritual self interprets and reacts to your intentions—or lack of intention. If you take responsibility for your health, your higher self engages more strongly with the healing process. Take stock of your life and health, and look at what you can do to improve your health and happiness. Take whatever action you can to help this happen. If you have serious health problems, this may seem like climbing a mountain. But any ascent begins with one small step upwards.

It may seem a strange thing to ask, but do you love yourself? This has nothing to do with being egotistical. Love of yourself is incredibly important spiritually. As we discussed earlier, if you express love towards yourself, a subtle change occurs in the water molecules of which your physical body is mainly comprised. They take on beautiful harmonious shapes. This indicates a positive reaction from your higher self. Self-love is paramount to your state of health. This will also attract the attention of your higher self into your life. Think about and express love to yourself as often as possible, and give yourself frequent hugs.

Engaging Your Higher Self

Your higher self is an integral part of your being. It is inside of you and all through you, above you and below you and all around you. It is a higher aspect of you and the great observer between and behind your thoughts. It is an intimate part of you. Connecting with your higher self is difficult to do directly. It lives intensely in the present, in the *now*. It does not communicate with language in the normal way. Its language is mental imagery, imagination, intention, and feeling. Affirmations are one way of getting a message across because they encapsulate intention and imagination and feeling in an active *now* tense.

Feeling and expressing love towards every aspect of yourself is a powerful way of engaging the higher aspects of yourself in your life. This is especially important to health and healing. Your higher self focuses on *your* focus, and the direction its energy moves in will always be aligned with your focus. But this can also work against you. If, for example, you have a damaged knee that causes pain and limitation, you naturally may focus on your pain and disability. You may just tolerate and ignore this condition. You may express anger and frustration towards your knee for failing you. These attitudes can direct your higher self to ignore your condition, or even to reinforce your pain and disability because this is what you are focusing upon. This is a bit like how a major cause of insomnia is the fear of not being able to sleep. (If you worry about not being able to sleep, you can manifest insomnia because that is your focus.)

To encourage your higher self to work for you, using the knee example, focus on loving your knee and imagining and seeing it as already being perfect in the *now*. This focus will engage your higher self to empower your body's innate self-healing power. Love yourself and love your knee. Imagine it already being perfect. Continually expect and look for improvements. Baby your knee, massage it and connect with it when it hurts, and pour your love into this perfect joint. Combined with energy work, this is an incredibly powerful healing operation.

How long it will take to heal anything has many variables and will usually happen in degrees. Use every little improvement to empower your healing intention. Do not allow yourself or others to talk negatively about your injury or problem. Many people are critical or *realistic* about such things. Realism is a good thing, but not when it comes to producing miracle healing. Contradictions will undermine your intentions and shift your focus back to reinforcing your pain and disability. Its difficult to change the way others think, so it is sometimes best to share what you are doing only with supportive people.

Energy and Self-Healing

Energy work and healing go hand in hand. No matter what healing modality is used, energy must pass through healers and into their patients. The more efficiently energy can flow through healers, the more beneficial will be the results. This also applies to healing yourself. The flow of healing energy combined with the healing intention is also a powerful way of engaging the assistance of your higher self in the healing act.

Novice healers should begin by practicing energy work and healing upon themselves. Self-healing is a voyage of discovery that not only repairs and rejuvenates the body and mind, but also alters your beliefs through experience. Spiritual development involves a series of realizations, and each realization arises through personal experience. This is a part of the process of getting in touch with your higher self and working in the greater spiritual reality.

Healing Affirmations

You create your own life and are the star of your own reality show. Get excited about this and the incredible possibilities that could manifest, including perfect health. This may sound like unrealistic or wishful thinking, but this is the best way to engage your higher self and invoke the law of attraction to make it actually happen in your life.

Before any self-healing or healing operation, formulate a specific intention to heal your body. Do not think about your injury or illness as it is now or how it used to be. Imagine your body as already being perfect in the *now*. Form a simple and clear affirmation and say this verbally or mentally several times as you begin. Say with conviction, "My body is perfect" or, "My knee is perfect" or, "My spine is perfect." Imagine, as strongly and as convincingly as you can to yourself, that your body is already perfect. This is your main focus and your intention, which you want to express to your higher self. Maintain this focus of intention as best you can throughout every day, and fall asleep with it on your mind.

Keep affirmations short and simple, active and present *now* tense. The higher self does not understand negatives and reversals of words. It does not understand past and future tense. It only understands the here and the *now*. So, affirmations must not read like, "I'm a *non-*smoker" or, "I do *not* smoke" because *non* and *not* will be misunderstood. The end result is reinforcement of the smoking habit. Instead, you could say, "I am free of nicotine" or, "I am smoke free" or, even better, "My lungs are clear and healthy." Imagine and feel that this is how they are *now*. When your higher self engages, it will do what it takes to manifest clear and healthy lungs in your body.

In the same way, a phrase like, "I do not have diabetes" can be misinterpreted. The affirmation, "I am healed of diabetes" is clearer. But even better, avoid the word "diabetes" entirely and say, "My blood is perfect in every way" or, "My pancreas is perfect in every way." These direct the attention of your higher self towards specific areas of your body that need healing, rather than towards the disease or problem. Through the law of attraction, you will attract exactly what you focus upon. So it is far better to focus clearly and specifically upon health and wealth rather than upon illness and debt.

Sleep Healing

Your body's natural self-repair and growth capabilities do most of their work while you sleep. The moments just prior to falling asleep provide a window of opportunity that can be used to empower self-healing. Body awareness actions develop a type of momentum and memory. They continue on their own even after you stop consciously performing them. This occurs even if you fall asleep while performing self-healing actions, as they will continue working while you sleep.

To perform sleep healing, focus on and express love and appreciation to yourself, especially sending love to the problem area you need to work upon. Imagine and feel this area as already being perfect. Then use suitable healing intentions and actions on this area. Continue doing this as you are falling asleep. The healing intention and action will continue while you sleep.

Energy work stimulates and refreshes the mind, and some people find that too much of it immediately before sleep can make falling asleep difficult. This affects some people more than others. Start with 10 minutes of energy work and if you sleep okay after this, then try 15, 20, et cetera.

Antiviral Self-Healing Boost

Energy work stimulates your body's self-healing systems. An important part of your body's self-healing system exists in the bone marrow within your thighbones. This produces cells that fight infection and disease in your body. Direct energy work on the thighbones stimulates bioelectrical activity there, which empowers this self-healing mechanism. A boost of vital energy is often all the physical body needs to defeat a virus. My explorations in this area have shown consistent results in hundreds of cases. This includes defeating common colds and influenza.

The first symptoms of the onset of influenza are sudden tiredness, sore throat, soreness in back of nasal passages, aching joints, and fever. The best chance of defeating influenza with energy work comes when the very first symptoms appear. This is when a virus is at its weakest and when you still have some vitality to fight it off. The body awareness antiviral method given below makes the best use of your remaining strength.

When cold or influenza strikes, as soon as you possibly can, take time out to do some emergency energy work—even if you have to sit in a washroom to get a break. Start by pre-stimulating your feet and legs. Formulate a self-healing intention and repeat the affirmation, "My body is perfect and healthy." Focus on your thighs. The area to work upon is between your knees and hip joints.

Focus awareness in your knees and create two electric blue energy balls there. Bounce these through your thighs back and forth between your knee and hip joints. Feel this action deep inside your thighs, inside the marrow of your thighbones. Increase the speed to a robust bounce action, about one-half second or less each way. Concentrate and put as much energy and attention into the bounce action as possible. Really *pump* the energy through your thighs for all you are worth. Thirty minutes of intense effort is recommended, but use whatever time is available.

If you cannot do this energy work immediately, do it as soon as you possibly can. Repeat this exercise as often as possible until all illness symptoms disappear. After this, remember to perform self-healing and intention while you are falling asleep so that the healing continues during sleep.

If everything goes according to plan, when you finish the emergency energy work, all illness symptoms will have vanished. However, the virus may fight back so be ready to repeat this as necessary. Do not accept the illness. Say the affirmation, "My body is perfectly healthy" over and over—and really mean it! Imagine, feel, and intend yourself as being perfectly healthy right *now*. This is also a good time to top up on vitamins and healthy juices and food. Do everything you possibly can that will help beat the virus.

If you do not catch a virus in time to defeat it immediately, please seek medical attention as you would normally. But do not give up on yourself. The effects and length of a virus can be reduced by continued effort and healthy intention.

Healing Physical Injuries

Physical pain activates your body's own biological self-repair and healing mechanisms, focusing these where they are needed. Body awareness energy work aids this process by directing and empowering these mechanisms. This is the essence of how all healing modalities work. They stimulate your body's own self-healing mechanisms.

Body awareness actions on bruised, swollen, or damaged body parts can sometimes cause temporary increases in pain. This is a natural response of your body's own self-healing mechanisms, which includes increased blood flow and nerve sensitivity. Pain killers are a blessing—but they can also slow the natural healing process.

Injuries such as sprained and bruised muscles, tendons, ligaments, and joints are where body awareness self-healing actions excel. In many cases, new injuries will heal overnight. The time needed to heal an injury will depend upon its severity and on the amount of self-healing energy work that is done. Long-term existing and recurring injuries will take longer to heal.

Note: The first action with any injury is to seek first aid and medical treatment.

Affirmation and Intention

Affirmation and intention aid the self-healing process by attracting the attention of your higher self to engage with the healing process. Let's use the example of self-healing an injured knee. Say and think, "My knee is perfect." Focus your body awareness senses on your knee and imagine you can see and feel a perfect knee joint. Express love and appreciation to your knee. Repeat this every time your knee spasms with pain. If you have continual pain, do this as frequently as possible.

Initial Energy Work Treatment

Again, we will use the example of an injured knee. After seeking first aid, focus body awareness on your injured knee. Use wrapping, brushing, stirring, sponging, and energy ball bounce actions on and through your knee. Also, occasionally bounce the whole leg with an energy ball during this treatment. Initially, spend about 30 minutes working on the new injury. Repeat this process as often as possible, and use the sleep healing method each night. The more energy work and self-healing done, the better your body's self-healing mechanisms will respond to repair the damage.

Extra Energy Tools

The energy tools introduced earlier can be used with good effect on physical injuries. Use whatever energy tools seem most appropriate. Start with the imaginary spray gun to wash the knee joint with the cooling water element. Imagine, feel, and intend this action to cool the joint and reduce inflammation and swelling. Then spray a cool, pale-blue healing foam and imagine this building up like shaving cream and soaking into the joint. Then pour brilliant fluid into the kneecap and imagine this soaking deeply into the joint. Finish by absorbing the earth element and filling the knee with this element to strengthen the joint.

Self-Healing Treatment

Sit, relax, and center yourself with awareness breathing. Pre-stimulate your hands and arms, and feet and legs, and then do a whole body bounce for a minute or two. Next, place your hands on or above the injured knee, close your eyes, and relax. As you breathe *in*, raise energy up your legs and torso to your heart primary center. As you breathe *out*, push the energy out through your arms and hands and into your injured knee. Continue this action over and over for several minutes or longer. Imagine your knee as being perfect as you do this.

Sleep Healing

When you go to bed, focus on the healing affirmation and intention, and then perform the initial energy work treatment actions given above for five minutes or more. Finish by using a wrapping action on the injured knee. Imagine you are wrapping the whole joint in a wide bandage and that the healing intention is being absorbed into the knee as it is wrapped. Continue this action as you fall asleep. In this way, it will continue while you are sleeping.

A little energy work prior to sleep is beneficial to general health and well-being, even if you only brush your feet for a minute or two. This will also increase the frequency and vividness of your dreams and lucid dreams. So, don't forget to brush your feet before you go to sleep.

When energy work and sleep healing are used, new sprains and sports-related injuries will often appear to heal unnaturally fast, sometimes overnight. However, even though the pain and swelling may be gone, the injured body part may not be fully healed. It may need more time to rest and recover fully before it can handle a full load. For this reason, it is wise to be cautious and not to overexert rapidly healed muscles, tendons, and joints too soon. Take it easy for a few days and do only light exercise. Increase this carefully until you are confident that the area will handle heavier physical activity.

Spinal Problems

Spinal problems generally respond well to body awareness and self-healing actions. This type of injury requires different actions and more work to get the best out of these methods. These actions will help with all types of spinal injuries, including disk and nerve damage. I can personally testify to the effectiveness of these methods, having had some fairly serious spinal injuries myself. Be proactive about your condition. Seek medical opinion and whatever alternatives are available to you. Miracles can and do happen.

Note: The first action after any spinal injury is to seek first aid and medical attention.

Spinal Affirmation and Intention

Say and think, "My spine is perfect" or, "My neck is perfect." Focus your body awareness senses in the damaged area of your spine. Imagine you can see and feel a perfect spine there. Express love and appreciation to your spine. Repeat this process every time your spine spasms or hurts. If you have constant pain, do this as frequently as possible and try to keep the healing intention in mind continually. This self-healing focus is essential for directing your higher self to engage in your healing. I cannot emphasize this part strongly enough; it is key. I know this is difficult if you are in a lot of pain, but try to be good humored and continue to heap love and appreciation onto your spine.

Spinal Treatment with Energy Tools

To perform spinal self-healing on yourself, lie on your back and make yourself comfortable. Place a pillow under your knees, as this will reduce the pressure on your lower spine. Relax and center yourself with awareness breathing. Carry out pre-stimulation exercises on your feet, legs, hands, and arms. Finish with a whole body bounce.

Focus body awareness on your tailbone. Imagine and feel an electric blue energy ball about the size of a tennis ball forming there.

Move the ball up through your spine to the top of the back of your head, and then back to your tailbone. Bounce the energy ball up and down, keeping the action focused in your spine. Take about one-half to one second each way. Next, focus the energy ball directly in the injured area. Move the energy ball up and down through the injury and several inches above and below. Next, use a side to side slicing action. Imagine a thin disk of shiny metal about five inches across. Start just below the injury and slice side to side through your spine. Move the disk a 16th of an inch (a few millimeters) up or down after every few slicing actions. Work your way slowly and thoroughly up and down through the whole injured area. Finish with a wrapping action as if you were wrapping a wide bandage around your spine (inside your body) and that this is covering and being absorbed into your spine. Continue each action for several minutes or more. You cannot overdo these actions.

(If your spinal injury is recent and inflammation and swelling are present, skip the flaming torch part given below and go directly to the spray gun water element. For new spinal injuries, the spray gun helps reduce inflammation and swelling. Add cooling and soothing properties to your intention.)

The next step is to use more energy tools. Start with your flaming torch. Apply this to the injured area with a suitably sized flame. Imagine and feel this is burning away damaged bone and scar tissue. Continue for a few minutes. Imagine ash and smoke appearing as damaged material is burned away. Next, tighten the flame to a white-hot cutting point and focus this directly in the injury. Imagine it penetrating deeply and dissolving scar tissue and damaged bone. Then use your spray gun to pour masses of the water element into the injury. Imagine this washing away damaged tissue and ash and cooling, soothing, and reducing inflammation. Continue for a few minutes or longer.

Next, imagine that the spray gun is producing mounds of cool, pale-blue, healing foam. Imagine this building up and soaking into the injury and rebuilding damaged bone and tissue. Continue for a few minutes. Pour brilliant fluid directly into the damaged area and imagine this soaking deeply into the vertebrae, disk, and nerves.

Continue for a few minutes or longer. Finish by absorbing the earth element into your spine to increase its strength.

Spinal Self-Healing Method

Lie on your back and relax and center yourself with awareness breathing. Pre-stimulate your hands and arms, and your feet and legs. Then do a whole body bounce for a minute or two. Place your hands on your stomach or neck, as close above the injured area as you can. Close your eyes and relax. You may not be able to actually touch the injured area, but you can direct the healing energy through your body to where it is needed.

As you breathe *in*, raise energy up your legs and torso to your heart primary center. As you breathe *out*, push the energy out through your arms and hands and into the injury. Imagine and feel the energy pouring into your spine. As you breathe the energy into the injury, say the words in your mind, "My spine is perfect." Continue this action with each breath for several minutes or longer. Imagine that your spine is perfect as you do this, and stay focused on your healing intention.

When you go to bed, focus on the healing affirmation and intention and perform the energy work actions given above for several minutes or so. Finish by using a wide wrapping action over the injured area of your spine. Continue this action as you fall asleep so it will continue through the night.

Caution: Do not overstress your spine after healing a new injury. Even if it stops hurting, your spine will require more time to strengthen before it will handle normal activity. Start with light exercise and build on this gradually. Continue the self-healing methods during recovery.

Stimulating Muscle, Nerve, and Bone Growth

Any injury can be helped with energy work, but conditions involving tissue, bone, nerve damage, and paralysis can take longer to heal. What can be done and how long it will take to get results will depend upon the age and extent of the injury. However, all of the body's self-repair systems can be stimulated into greater activity with energy work. In this respect, energy work can be likened to a kind of internal body awareness physiotherapy.

When imaginary activities are performed, the same motor centers and nerves in the physical brain and body activate as when they are physically performed. This factor is utilized in sports psychology, where athletes repeatedly imagine themselves performing their sport. This is shown to improve physical performance during the actual sporting events. This same principle, imagining physical activity and exercise, has also been shown to improve the condition of the muscles of body parts that have been immobilized for a long time, paralyzed, or in plaster casts.

The above explanation relates to the underlying principles of how body awareness tactile imaging works, and is what causes energy movement sensations. The localized application of energy work and tools to injuries stimulates the body's self-repair systems more strongly than does imagination alone. This improves circulation and encourages bone, tissue, nerve, and muscle growth. The examples given earlier involving a damaged knee and spine show the types of actions that are needed to accomplish this.

When a body part becomes paralyzed, it soon fades into the background and is eventually forgotten. It is normal to focus on what works and to ignore what does not work. While accepting something that cannot be changed is realistic, this acceptance can work against the self-healing process. An injured, paralyzed, or dysfunctional body part needs to be highlighted, loved, and appreciated. Accept what is, but improvement should be always expected.

The energy work actions and tools used, plus the affirmations and intentions and imagination components, will need adjusting to suit your particular circumstances and injuries. For example, if you have a damaged spinal cord in your neck, first check your X-rays so you can identify the exact site of the damage. Then use all of the energy work actions and tools on this area.

First use the self-healing method, raising energy to your heart on the *in* breath and pumping energy into your injury on the *out* breath. Then bounce an energy ball up and down through the damaged area. Focus this in the spine itself and not on the whole throat. Also use the slicing action: Imagine a small, metal disk the size of a drink coaster. Slice this side to side through your neck. Shift this action a sixteenth of an inch up or down after every few slices. Start just below the injury and work your way thoroughly up and down through the damaged area. Repeat with a back and forth slicing action. Then use a wrapping action on the injured area.

Next use energy tools, starting with the flaming torch, to burn away damaged bone and scar tissue. As you do this, imagine your spine and spinal cord as being perfect while you burn everything else away. Pour brilliant fluid into the injury. Use the spray gun to wash away debris and toxic energy and to cool the area. Finish by spraying the area with lots of pale-blue, healing foam. Do this several times a day, and use the wrapping action while you are falling asleep.

The affirmations for a neck injury would be, "My spine is perfect" or, "My neck is perfect" or, "My spinal cord is perfect," or all three. Always imagine your spine and spinal cord as already being perfect. Express love and appreciation to your neck. All of these things will help to engage your higher self in the self-healing process.

Body Awareness Exercises

For paralyzed and wasted muscles, it can help if you imagine and feel yourself exercising them several times a day. This will encourage nerves and muscles to strengthen and repair themselves. The type of exercise will vary depending on the injury. Start with something simple, like imagining and feeling each leg and arm rising one at a time. Close your eyes and imagine and feel this as strongly as possible with body awareness and without physically moving. Exercise each of your disabled body parts in this way, with simple imagined lifting and stretching. When you get used to this, add something more complex like imagining yourself jogging, swimming, et cetera.

Self-Healing Tumors and Diseased Organs

The principles of treating diseased organs and tumors are similar to any other type of energy work self-healing. With diseased or dysfunctional organs, energy work and tools need to be focused at the problem site. Check with an anatomy chart to make sure you know exactly where the problem tumor or organ is situated.

Tumors

Use the energy work and tools as you would for any injury. When you use the energy work tools on a tumor, however, imagine the tumor being destroyed by the energy tools. Imagine it being ripped out with the iron tongs, burned away by the flaming torch, scooped away with the golden net, washed away with the spray gun, et cetera. Then spend time imagining the area as being perfect and completely without the tumor. Using a breast tumor as an example, express love and appreciation to your breast. The affirmations and intentions used should *not* reflect the existence of a tumor. Instead, imagine your breast as being perfect and beautiful inside and out and say, "My breast is perfect."

Dysfunctional Organs

Use the energy work, self-healing, and energy tools as you would for any injury. Focus energy work actions and tools in and around the dysfunctional organ. To work on dysfunctional kidneys, for example, you would bounce energy balls through them, then burn away toxic energy with the flaming torch, then spray massive amounts of water into them, and then lots of pale-blue, healing foam. The kidneys filter impurities and fluids from the blood and produce urine, so this organ's function involves water. As such, pouring large amounts of water element into it is beneficial. The affirmations and intentions used should reflect perfect water functionality. Imagine your kidneys as being perfect in every way. Say, "My kidneys are perfect." Also, imagine that your kidneys are absorbing the water element and pouring frothy, yellow urine into your bladder while you repeat the affirmation, "My perfect kidneys filter water." Imagine they are already perfect in the *now*.

Empowered Belief

Empowered belief is an essential component for manifesting miracle self-healing. Use the energy work exercises and self-healing methods and energy tools frequently. Imagine that your injured or dysfunctional body part is perfect with all your heart. Express love and appreciation to your body as strongly as you can, particularly to the problem area. Hold the affirmation and the image of perfection in your mind as powerfully as you can and as often as you can. Go to sleep with this on your mind and wake up each morning expecting improvement. *Never give up.* Miracles do happen.

Practice

Close your eyes, relax, and center yourself with awareness breathing. Pre-stimulate the hands and arms, and the feet and legs, and then finish with a whole body bounce.

Perform the antiviral action. Focus on your thighs and create energy balls in your knees. Move these from your knees to your hip joints, bouncing them back and forth. Feel the energy balls moving through the whole of your thighs, deep inside the bone marrow of your thighbones, as keenly as you can. Increase the bounce speed to one-half second or less each way. Continue this powerfully for five minutes or more.

Focus on a damaged joint, if you have one, or focus on a knee. Bounce an energy ball through the joint from several directions, and then use the metal disk slicing action side to side and then back and forth. Use the flaming blowtorch, then the golden net, and then use the spray gun with water and then with pale-blue, healing foam. Insert energy needles and pour brilliant fluid into the joint. Absorb the earth element and feel this filling your leg and strengthening your knee. Finish by wrapping the knee with an imaginary bandage and feeling this soaking into the joint.

This chapter has taught many practical healing uses for energy work and tools. Coming up next, we build on this by showing you how to help other people with these skills and how to project energy for contact and distance healing.

EIGHT

Heart Center Healing

Giving healing to other people is not difficult. You have already practiced the necessary skills to do this. The basic healing act involves raising and projecting healing energy into another person. It can also involve using the energy tools we have been working with to target specific areas of the body to stimulate healing responses. Giving healing regularly is also the best spiritual development practice I know. This helps both healers and their patients.

I have been a healer for more than 30 years. I have often been asked what healing is and how it works. I struggled with these questions from the very beginning and have thought about them a great deal over the years. The explanations given by healers and spiritual teachers on the how and why of healing vary greatly. Explanations are relative, shaped by the background and training and the personal experiences and beliefs of the healer or teacher in question.

José's Tale

One of my very first patients in the mid-1970s was a 12-year-old boy, José. He was going blind from an incurable congenital eye condition. José was the first person to pose these questions to me. I answered him as best I could, and after hearing my somewhat confusing explanations, I think José got the impression that I was some kind of angelic undercover agent. However, something must have worked because my explanation seemed to make sense to José. After his first healing session, he demonstrated unyielding faith that he would be healed.

After his second weekly visit, José hid his very thick and expensive glasses and refused to wear them—much to the distress of his parents. He said that he could see much better without them. I got a frantic phone call from his mother, asking me to convince José to wear his glasses. When I saw José for his third visit, I raised the subject. He was adamant that he could see better without the glasses, but that his mother did not believe him. I believed him and encouraged him, while also trying to placate his mother. José struggled with poor vision at school, but his great faith was soon rewarded.

On his fourth weekly visit, José marched proudly into my healing sanctuary with sparkling eyes and an awestruck mother in tow. He gave me an enthusiastic hug and generally bounced about the room. They had come directly from an appointment with his eye specialist. The tests showed that José now had perfect 20/20 vision. José's eye specialist was, like his mother, speechless. The reversal of José's congenital eye condition could not be explained.

The next time I saw José was 25 years later. It was wonderful to see him again. He now has a family of his own and works as an electrician. José is adored as a husband and father, and he still has 20/20 vision. A patient's faith in his or her recovery is like pure gold to any doctor or healer.

When I first started giving healing, I worked intuitively and never gave the how and why of it much thought. It was a bit like trying to hatch an egg. I would relax and try to put myself into an altered state and fill my mind with healing intention. I would then put my hands on my patients and hope and pray for some kind of tingling spiritual energy flow. This usually worked, but I did not understand what was happening. If it did not work, there was nothing I could do to make it happen. Since then, though, my exploration of the energy body has provided me with considerable insight into these things.

Now matter how it's described, healing essentially comes from the heart and involves a spiritual act of mature compassion. It can aptly be said that a healer's higher self engages the patient's higher self to trigger a healing response. At the most basic level, diseased and dysfunctional areas of the energy body can be said to contain too little positive energy or too much negative energy. A flow of healing energy triggers a healing response that replenishes distorted or blocked areas of the patient's energy body. This has a healing effect upon the patient's physical body by triggering and empowering the patient's own biological self-healing mechanisms.

Healing Method

My healing method engages the entire energy body, but the heart primary center is key. An energy pumping action is used to raise energy up through the body to the heart center, and then to push it out through the arms and into the patient. This action alone will produce a beneficial level of healing energy. It also causes the heart center to begin accumulating energy. When this reaches a critical point, the heart center will strobe and release a strong, pulsing flow of healing energy on the primary center level. This whole body almost orgasmic pulsing energy surge can aptly be described as a Kundalini-related phenomenon.

Please understand that a heart center strobe is definitely not necessary for effective healing. The act of healing can involve different configurations of primary centers and spiritual development and healing energy frequency attunements. Some healers experience similar things to the heart center strobe I describe, including warm tingling flows of energy up through the back and arms or down through the head, neck, and arms. These all involve higher primary centers, and all involve the heart primary center.

I have spoken to many healers from a good variety of healing traditions over the years. Most healers feel some kind of energy flow, which relates to the heart center. Typically, healers feel a tingling energy flow up their backs, down through their heads, or both. The strength of these sensations varies from light to heavy. Some healers experience things like the heart center strobe I describe here. Some people can turn healing on and off at will, like throwing a switch, and stand there chatting while they give healing. There are many different styles and ways of giving healing that produce effective healing energy of various frequencies. Some of these methods can be learned from a book whereas some, like Reiki, require a hands-on attunement from an established practitioner. (An attunement involves experiencing a healing energy frequency so one can then tune into the same source of healing energy.)

With the heart center method, practical healing and energy work experience may be required before one acquires the ability to experience a heart center strobe. How long this takes will vary from healer to healer and depends upon development work and natural ability. Beneficial healing can be given with the heart center healing method even though it may not strobe noticeably. Combined with regular meditation, energy work, and healing practice, this healing method *will* develop healing ability. The healing act engages the attention of the higher self and exposes healers to powerful currents of healing energy. This attention and exposure cause spiritual development.

In my case, it took a year or so of alternating daily between doing altered state meditation and development work, and giving regular healing, before my heart center began strobing during the healing act. This was intermittent at first, and I did not understand what was happening. This steadily became more dependable, though, and eventually became a major part of every healing I performed. A full heart center strobe is a powerful but pleasant phenomenon. Most of the energy is felt moving up through the back to the heart primary center, and then down through the arms. The rear parts of primary centers are heavily involved with the healing act.

The amount of preparation and energy work a healer needs before a healing session varies with experience. When I first started,

I took 15 minutes of quiet time to prepare myself. I still do this if I have a number of people to heal, although I can now enter the healing state in a few seconds. I recommend that new healers spend at least a few minutes preparing themselves before a healing session. The most important thing for a healer to achieve before healing is a relaxed and centered state.

Healing can be performed in any situation, but it is more powerful if some time is spent preparing. Sit, relax, and center yourself with awareness breathing. Pre-stimulate your feet and legs, and your hands and arms, and then finish with a whole body bounce. Return to awareness breathing for a minute or two to deepen your level of relaxation. Feel yourself falling into yourself, moving deeper and deeper as if you were in an elevator going down. Then begin the healing and try to maintain this relaxed state throughout. With time and practice, you will find yourself shifting into the healing state more quickly.

Healing can be done sitting or standing. When you are ready to begin, have your patient sit within easy reach in front or to the side of you, or you may stand behind them. Ask them to close their eyes, relax, and remain silent until you have finished. It is important to stop chatter as this can break a healer's focus, which is a delicate state. Close your eyes and take a couple of deep breaths to relax for a few moments. Say a simple prayer for your patient or an affirmation to express the healing intention. Keep this short and simple and present active tense, reflecting the patient's condition as already being healed: "This body is perfect" or "This spine is perfect" or "This organ is perfect." Hold the healing intention and imagine the patient as being perfectly healthy. Keep your mind as clear of thought words as possible. The energy work pumping action will help keep your mind focused.

The healing act involves not only energy flow, but also an empathic or psychic healer-patient attunement. A connection forms between healer and patient and between the healer's higher self and the patient's higher self. The healing state of focus and intention does not involve words. Wordlessly express your compassion and desire to heal. Feel this like a peaceful, loving emotion gently welling up inside of you. Feel compassion but hold yourself beyond any pain, distress, and emotional turmoil that your patient may be experiencing so you are not distracted from your task.

I normally sit side on to my patient and place my left hand over the back of their head and my right hand over their heart or brow. I then move my hands over the body, an inch or so above my patient, not touching. I often find warm, cool, or tingling patches. These are areas needing attention, so I let my hand rest there a while and pump some healing energy there before moving on. I finish by returning my hands to my patient's head and heart. You do not have to physically touch a patient to give healing. Some healers prefer to hold their hands several inches or more away from their patients. I prefer to lay my hands on my patients because this adds a level of intimacy that I feel improves my connection with them.

When you are ready to give healing, draw energy up from both feet and legs, up through your torso and back, and into your heart primary center on the *in* breath. On the *out* breath, push the energy out through your shoulders and arms and into your patient. Your breathing will help you regulate this energy pumping action. In time this will become almost automatic. Imagine your body is a big X, with the

Out breath

In breath

center of the X being your heart and the extenders being your arms and legs.

- During the in breath, draw energy up from your feet, legs, torso, and back and into your heart center. Then hold your body awareness focus in your heart as you continue breathing energy into your heart as you finish the whole *in* breath.
- During the whole *out* breath, push energy from your heart out through your shoulders, down your arms, and into your patient. Hold your body awareness focus in your arms and feel as if you are breathing the energy into your patient through your arms and hands. Continue this for the duration of the whole *out* breath. Repeat this action over and over. Breathe deeply and regularly, and create a smooth body awareness pumping action. You will quickly develop a feel for this.

Continue the energy pumping action throughout the healing act with each patient. If your heart center does not strobe, continue this for several minutes or as long as desired. When your heart center does strobe, tingling waves of energy will be felt pulsing up your back, down through your arms, and into your patient. This is a noticeable tingling, pumping sensation. You may also feel tingling energy flowing automatically down through your head.

When your heart center strobes, the intensity of your breathing will increase and you may find yourself panting for a short time. Relax and go with this, as heavy breathing will help you pump more energy into your patient. It is important to stay in control and not to allow yourself to be overcome by these powerful sensations. Just let it happen and go with the flow.

Avoid giving diagnoses and prognoses of patients' conditions, and do not give medical advice. I have seen many fine healers discredit themselves in this way. A healer's task is to give healing, not a psychic reading or diagnosis. If patients ask for an opinion, tell them that you strongly believe that their health will improve, but by how much is unknown. As a healer, you have to believe in this with all your heart. If you can pass on this expectation to patients, so much the better. However, a healer cannot promise anything.

Many patients appear to fall asleep during healing. But if they were alone in the room sitting in a hard chair, they would not be able to fall asleep. The healing attunement will often draw patients into altered states of consciousness because of the close empathic/psychic connection they have with their healers and the joint higher self connection.

If your brow and crown centers become involved in the healing act, visions and psychic impressions can manifest. These will usually relate to the patient on hand. Whether or not you relate what you perceive at the time is up to you. This depends on how much time is available and how many patients you have waiting. A healer's purpose is to give healing and nothing more. Sharing will erode your relaxed and attuned state. Anything notable can be passed onto patients after the healing session is completely finished.

A heart center strobe is a pumping, tingling, semi-orgasmic feeling that rises in intensity and then fades over several seconds. You will feel the energy pumping through your back and down your arms. The intensity of this is affected by the development of the healer and the needs of the patient. Episodes of heart center strobing can occur once or several times during a single healing act. More heart center strobes can be produced by continuing the pumping action, but these are generally less intense than the first.

Distance Healing

The heart center healing method can also be used for distance healing. A letter, photograph, or email letter can be used to make the healer/patient connection. If you have personally met the patient, this will also help create a good connection.

Any kind of real-time connection will improve the act of distance healing. A telephone conversation or instant messaging chat session will provide the best connections. A small lock of hair or similar, combined with a photograph, also provides a good connection for distance healing.

To perform distance healing, sit in a quiet place and prepare yourself in the same way you would for contact healing. Hold the letter or picture or place it before you, or sit in front of your PC with the letter or picture onscreen. If connected via telephone or Internet chat, ask patients to close their eyes, relax, and be silent. The same basic technique is used for distance healing as is for contact healing. When you are ready to begin, imagine that your patient's head is within easy arm's reach. Then reach out and place your hands (your real physical hands) where you imagine your patient's head to be. Perform the energy pumping action through your heart primary center, exactly as you would do during contact healing.

Distance healing can occur in real time or in nonlinear time. Sometimes patients will feel your hands on them while you are giving them healing and/or the energy of the healing act. But sometimes patients will feel the healing energy arrive many hours or even days later. This is variable and of no real concern, as long as the healing gets through to the patient.

A computer is a wonderful help for distance healing. I have three folders on my computer for this purpose. The first holds photographs of the people I am actively working upon. I set up a slide show, dim the lights, prepare myself, and then start the slide show and give healing to each person as their picture appears on my screen. The second folder is for people I am working with long term. These faces are in my memory so I give these people healing by remembering the folder pictures and imagining their faces and conditions. I sometimes give healing to the entire folder if I am short on time. The third is a holding folder for people I have lost touch with. Regular progress reports are necessary to continue distance healing. If I do not hear from a patient in a month, I shift their picture into my holding area.

Using Energy Tools for Contact and Distance Healing

All of the energy tools and self-healing procedures and elements given earlier can be used to help other people (and animals) for both contact and distance healing. This can be time-consuming, but it is extremely effective. I use a combination of these methods, first giving heart center healing, and then using elements and energy tools, et cetera.

For contact healing, first use the heart center healing method, and then use energy tools and elements as you would for self-healing, but shift the focus of these into your patient. The more time you spend doing this the better will be the results.

At some time during every contact or distance healing act, mentally express love and appreciation to your patient and affirm and imagine your patient and their disorder as being perfect. I always say, "*I love you*" as powerfully as I can in my mind several times, and I imagine my patient's condition as being perfect. I can feel my higher self engage in this.

For distance healing, imagine that your patient is standing before you if you are sitting or floating above you if you are in bed. Imagine that you can see inside your patient's body to the problem area. Give heart center healing, and then use the other healing procedures and energy tools to treat your patient's problem. Finish by affirming and imagining your patient's disorder as being perfect.

An interesting phenomenon can occur from time to time during distance healing. Sometimes the patient will appear before you, seen clairvoyantly in your mind's eye. You may see persons as they would look normally or you may see inside their bodies, their internal organs laid bare and problem areas highlighted in color. I think this phenomenon results from using such specific healing intentions, say to work on a patient's kidneys or heart. Because this intention is so focused on a patient's internal organs, the higher self responds by showing you what you are focusing upon. When this happens, the connection and healing experience are always profound.

Releasing Energy Cords

Both contact and distance healing involve temporary energy connections forming between healers and patients. This applies to all healing modalities and not just the methods given here. These connections usually dissolve after a healing session, but sometimes this does not happen. Energy cords can then form, connecting healers with the underlying spiritual and energetic problems of their patients. These cords can adversely affect the life and health of a healer, particularly when such cords have been allowed to accumulate.

To overcome this problem, dissolving connections and *releasing* patients from your space is recommended at the end of each healing act. This is quickly and easily done. In your mind's eye, imagine your patient floating before you, bathed in brilliant light. Mentally state the firm command "I revoke all connections and release you from my space." Then imagine your patient shrinking away and happily dissolving into the light. This clearly demonstrates to your higher self that you do not wish any energy connection with this person to continue outside the healing session.

Releasing energy cords helps enormously, but some healers and patients are just not compatible because of energetic and spiritual conflicts. This will usually be obvious during or after the first session, whether contact or distance healing is involved. The healer will not feel comfortable with the healer/patient connection. The healer should then politely withdraw and release the client, possibly redirecting him or her to another healer.

Finally, if you ever experience adverse side-effects during or after a healing session, perform a shower and/or salt bath energy dump, as explained earlier, with the firm intention of washing away any energy connections that might have formed. If you do a lot of healing, a daily shower energy dump is highly recommended.

Energy Work and Traditional Practices

Regardless of previous training, body awareness energy work can be integrated into or used to improve any traditional style or practice. This is a universal method for stimulating and developing the human energy body. Enhanced sensitivity and increased energy flow will improve any energy related or spiritual practice. This also applies to different healing systems. Energy work and healing are intimately connected. No matter what is believed or which modality is used, energy must pass through the healer and into the patient. The more efficiently this is accomplished, the more beneficial will be the results.

Some people prefer to learn and practice body awareness energy work separately from their original practices. This is workable, as body awareness energy work conditions and sensitizes the energy body to a higher energy flow, which automatically enhances any practice or style. The ideas and methods presented here can be used for a stand-alone practice or to enhance any traditional practices. The most important thing is to do what works for you; remember that what works, works.

A Few Last Words

If you step back a little and look at how your energy body affects you, some questions will arise that beg to be answered. The functioning of your energy body profoundly affects your entire state of being on all levels: physically, emotionally, mentally, and spiritually. There is no escaping this: you are your energy body and your energy body is you. These are indivisible aspects of yourself. Your state of being and living flows from the wellspring of your energy body. Your energy body is also your strongest and most direct personal link to your spiritual roots. So, if you aspire to spiritual development, realization, and enlightenment, there is really nowhere else to look but within yourself.

As should be clear after reading my book, beneath your physical body is a complex, layered, subtle energy field that is popularly called the energy body. This exists only one small step away from your physical body, an inward step which brings you ever closer to your spiritual roots. Your energy body is your own personal connection with everything—within yourself and with the greater spiritual reality as a whole. It does not matter how you label these greater spiritual aspects of being. Look no further than within if you want to connect with and begin to realize these.

Your mind and spirit are intimately enmeshed within your own physical body. Take this as a given and it becomes obvious that this way can also provide you with personal access to the great divine. Nowhere else are the higher spiritual and divine aspects of yourself closer or more reachable than within. Nothing else outside of you could be closer to this simple truth.

At every class I teach, I ask my students to raise a finger and physically point to where God is, and then to point to where God is not. These are both impossible tasks, but this is an excellent demonstration of a simple but profound truth. God exists as much inside of you as outside of you. And if you consider that this also applies to every living being, thing, plant, rock, and atom in the universe, then you will have a glimpse of your divine connectedness with the universe and the greater reality. This includes all things individually and collectively. Your separation from everything outside of yourself is a grand illusion. The realization of your all-encompassing connectedness with everything and everyone is truly illuminating, in every sense of the word.

The path to discovering truth and enlightenment is too simple for most people to grasp. It is usually the last thing considered, and after every other possibility has been explored and discarded. The secret is that your higher self and everything divine is closer and more directly approachable and reachable within your own self in the here and now. To tread this path, your attention must be directed into your own body and mind, into your own self, and into your life.

Your body, mind, and spirit form an inseparable unity during your physical existence. Your physical body is intimately enmeshed with every level of your spirit and your mind: conscious, subconscious, and superconscious. These aspects cannot be separated. Your closest and most direct link to the divine and the greater spiritual reality is therefore *through your own body and self.* Raise a finger and point to another source that is closer, clearer, or more within your own personal reach.

The roots of body awareness tactile imaging energy work can be found in most Eastern and Western spiritual practices, although the connection is often not apparent. From ancient Zen and Taoist teachings to contemporary spiritual teachers like Eckhart Tolle, the importance of body awareness, of going within, of self-observation, of knowing yourself, and of living in the present here and now comes through loud and clear.

Eckhart Tolle is the author of *The Power of NOW: A Guide to Spiritual Enlightenment* and other books, essential reading for all who aspire towards spiritual development. After reading my book, the instructions Tolle gives in *The Power of NOW* may sound hauntingly familiar. Tolle instructs his readers to focus attention within, to focus body awareness on different parts of the body in order to energetically stimulate those parts. While the same principles apply, I teach a more systematic approach to energy work. I would similarly instruct you first on how to focus your body awareness effectively. You would then use body awareness actions to pre-stimulate your feet and legs, hands and arms, and then perform a whole body bounce action—*feeling* this moving up and down through your whole body. Tolle uses different terminology, but we are saying much the same thing.

Body awareness tactile imaging energy work provides tools that will help reconnect you with your inner self. These tools will help you to personally explore and develop your own subtle energy body and beyond. This will not only improve your health and well-being, but it will also put you in touch with your higher spiritual aspects. And the more aware you become of your physical body, mind, and inner self, the more your higher spiritual self—*The Great I Am* within you—will become aware of you.

Bibliography and Suggested Reading

Arntz, William, Betsy Chasse, and Mark Vicente. *What the Bleep Do We Know!?: Discovering the Endless Possibilities for Altering Your Everyday Reality.* FL, HCI Inc., 2005.

Bardon, Franz. *Initiation into Hermetics.* Salt Lake City UT, Merkur Pub. Co., 2001.

Brennan, Barbara Anne. *Hands of Light: A Guide to Healing Through the Human Energy Field.* New York NY, Bantam, 1988.

Bruce, Robert. *Astral Dynamics: A NEW Approach to Out-of-Body Experience.* Charlottesville VA, Hampton Roads, 1999.

——. *Practical Psychic Self-Defense: Understanding and Surviving Unseen Influences.* Charlottesville VA, Hampton Roads, 2002.

——, and Brian Mercer. *Mastering Astral Projection: 90-Day Guide to Out-of-Body Experience.* Woodbury MN, Llewellyn Worldwide, 2004.

Byrne, Rhonda. *The Secret.* Hillsboro OR, Beyond Words, 2006.

Caruso, Andrew. *Sports Psychology Basics.* Indianapolis IN, Reedswain, 2004.

Coelho, Paulo. *The Alchemist.* CA, HarperSanFrancisco, 2006.

Deadman, Peter, Kevin Baker, and Mazin Al-Khafaji. *A Manual of Acupuncture.* Seattle WA, Eastland Press, 1998.

Emoto, Masaru. *Love Thyself: The Message from Water 3.* Carlsbad CA, Hay House, 2006.

———, and David A. Thayne. *The Hidden Messages in Water.* Markham Ontario, Atria, 2005.

Gerber, Richard. *Vibrational Medicine: The #1 Handbook of Subtle-Energy Therapies.* Rochester VT, Bear and Co., 2001.

Gopi Krishna. *Higher Consciousness and Kundalini.* Ontario, F.I.N.D. Research Trust, 1993.

Gordon, Richard and C. Norman Shealy. *Quantum-Touch: The Power to Heal.* Berkeley CA, North Atlantic Books, 2006.

Iovine, John. *Kirlian Photography: A Hands-On Guide.* NY, Images Publishing, 2000.

Lindgren, C. E. *Capturing the Aura: Integrating Science, Technology and Metaphysics.* Nevada City NV, Blue Dolphin, 2000.

McTaggart, Lynne. *The Field: The Quest for the Secret Force of the Universe.* London, Element, 2003.

Oschman, James L. and Candace Pert. *Energy Medicine: The Scientific Basis.* London, Churchill Livingstone, 2000.

Pert, Candace B. *Molecules of Emotion: The Science Behind Mind-Body Medicine.* New York NY, Simon & Schuster, 1999.

Ramtha (J. Z. Knight). *A Beginner's Guide to Creating Reality (Third Edition).* Yelm WA, JTZ Pub., 2004.

Tolle, Eckhart. *The Power of NOW: A Guide to Spiritual Enlightenment.* London, Hodder and Stroughton, 2001.

———. *The New Earth: Awakening to Your Life's Purpose.* Toronto ON, Plume, 2006.

Tung-Pin, Lu (Richard Wilhelm, translator). *The Secret of the Golden Flower: A Chinese Book of Life.* Fort Washington PA, Harvest Book Co., 1962.

Tzo Kuo, Shih and Charles Stein. *Qi Gong Therapy: The Chinese Art of Healing with Energy.* NY, Station Hill Press, 1994.

Wilkinson, Richard H. and Richard H. Wilk. *Symbol & Magic in Egyptian Art.* London, Thames and Hudson, 1999.

Index

Robert Bruce is a true spiritual pioneer of our times. Author of five groundbreaking books, his life is spent exploring the dynamics of all things paranormal and spiritual, and testing the boundaries of the greater reality. This exploration particularly involves the human energy body, which is the foundation of both physical and spiritual existence and the interactive key to all spiritual exploration. The depth and scope of Robert's experiential knowledge is remarkable. Robert's other areas of expertise include astral projection, kundalini phenomena, minds-eye vision, spiritual and psychic development, metaphysics, and psychic self-defense. Robert is a man who lives in the greater reality and asks others to join him. Robert lectures internationally and currently lives in Australia. You can find him on the Web at www.astraldynamics.com.

Hampton Roads Publishing Company

. . . for the evolving human spirit

HAMPTON ROADS PUBLISHING COMPANY publishes books
on a variety of subjects, including metaphysics, spirituality,
health, visionary fiction, and other related topics.

For a copy of our latest trade catalog, call toll-free,
800-766-8009, or send your name and address to:

HAMPTON ROADS PUBLISHING COMPANY, INC.
1125 STONEY RIDGE ROAD • CHARLOTTESVILLE, VA 22902
e-mail: hrpc@hrpub.com • www.hrpub.com